D0209388

CALGARY PUBLIC LIBRARY

How to Survive Christmas

How to Survive Christmas

Jilly Cooper

**An Xmasochist's guide to the
darkest days of the year**

with drawings by Timothy Jaques

METHUEN

Other books by Jilly Cooper
published by Methuen

JOLLY SUPER

JOLLY SUPER TOO

JOLLY SUPERLATIVE

SUPERJILLY

SUPERCOOPER

JOLLY MARSUPIAL

CLASS

INTELLIGENT AND LOYAL

SUPER MEN AND SUPER WOMEN

WORK AND WEDLOCK

THE COMMON YEARS

The lines of poetry on page 25 are from 'Christmas shopping', from *The Collected Poems of Louis MacNeice*, edited by E. R. Dodds, and are reproduced by kind permission of Faber and Faber Ltd. The lines on page 91 are from 'Christmas', from John Betjeman's *Collected Poems* and are reproduced by kind permission of John Murray Ltd.

First published in Great Britain in 1986
by Methuen London Ltd
11 New Fetter Lane, London EC4P 4EE
Copyright © 1986 by Jilly Cooper
Illustrations copyright © 1986 by Timothy Jaques

Made and printed in Great Britain
by Richard Clay (The Chaucer Press) Ltd,
Bungay, Suffolk

ISBN 0 413 59780 6

to William and Susannah Franklyn
with love

Contents

Acknowledgements   8

Introduction   11

One: Christmas is Coming   17

Two: Bearing Gifts We Traverse Too Far   47

Three: The Dark Night Wakes, The Glory Breaks   81

Four: But What Comes After . . .   111

Five: We Make the Golden Journey to Samarkand   133

Left-overs   139

Acknowledgements

Being a lousy cook, a rotten planner, and the worst wrapper of presents in recorded history, my only real qualification for writing this book is that I have the example of my brilliant husband, Leo, who is not only an ace cook, but, having been in the Army, knows all about organisation and delegation. I also have some marvellous friends, who with true Christmas spirit came up with countless anecdotes and ideas.

They include: Ewa Lewis, Roger and Rowena Luard, Rosemary and David Nolan, Candida Crewe, Christopher Chamberlain, Susannah Franklyn, Bob Kay, Susan Kyle, Jennifer Sherborne, Christopher Moorsom, Angela Sallitt, Pegotty Henriques, Rosie Cheltenham, David D'Eath, Antonia Hunt, Tita Carter, Lesley Garner, Don Grant, Adrian and Felicity Rowbotham, Carole Taylor and Johanna Powell.

I should also like to thank my publishers, Geoffrey Strachan and Anne Askwith, for editing the book, and Annalise Kay and Beryl Hill, for so nobly typing the manuscript.

Introduction

A few years ago on *Woman's Hour*, I heard a farmer complaining about the cruel way in which he was compelled to rear turkeys. Because the housewife wanted a cheap Christmas dinner, the wretched birds were force-fed, and put on weight so quickly that they had to stagger round on legs too weak to support their vast bulk, and often had heart attacks long before Christmas. He was caught in a trap, the farmer explained, because he needed the money, and if he didn't rear turkeys in this way, other farmers would.

Ever since, I have been haunted by this image of the farmer and his turkeys. It seems to symbolise today's family – particularly the housewife – staggering under the unnecessary toil and financial pressures of Christmas, which should be a season of love and joy, but which many of us dread, feeling only passionate relief when it's all over.

The reason for this, I think, is that Christmas goes on too long. Not only does the entire country grind to a halt for a fortnight over the actual holiday, but Christmas starts in the shops in September, so that by the time you get to 25 December you're absolutely fed up to the walnut-filled cavities with the whole thing.

Matters are not helped by journalists – me included – who not only have to write their Christmas pieces weeks, or even months, before Christmas week and before the full horror has started, but who are all so frantic for a new angle that they make their readers feel madly guilty if they are not disguising unsightly loo chains with homemade tinsel, and fricassee-ing burst balloons and cracker mottoes on Boxing Day.

Christmas is also an uneasy mingling of festivals. Originally, mid-winter and the return of the sun after the shortest day were celebrated by a prolonged booze-up, a mixture of the Roman Saturnalia and the German Yule, in which people decked their houses with evergreens, exchanged presents, visited friends and generally made merry. It was only later, in about the fourth century AD, that this mid-winter holiday was chosen as the most suitable time to celebrate the birth of Christ, with its message of peace on earth and looking after those less fortunate than ourselves.

The conflict thus comes because we feel that we deserve – like the early Romans – to be enjoying ourselves and having a blow-out, but feel – like the early Christians – that we ought to be doing good to others at the same time. Alas, those we should invite to spend Christmas with us – widowed Rich Great Aunt Phyllis who grumbles all the time or the lonely friendless colleague at work – are often the people who bore and irritate us the most.

Stress is also added these days because so many people are out of work; and the only thing most of them can afford to do over Christmas is to watch television, which bombards them with images of plenty and exhortations to spend more and more. But Christmas in any family is a time of financial pressure, when breadwinners feel they are falling short. Any family can do without a holiday, or a new carpet, or central heating, but at Christmas, because everyone is doing more or less the same thing at the same time, comparisons are inevitable. If you can't afford a turkey, a tree or presents, you can't run and hide. This applies whether you are on the breadline in Belfast, or being badgered by your wife in Belgravia to give a party for 300.

One comfort, however, despite the journalists' constant harking back to the good, old, simple, non-commercial days, is that nothing has really changed. Thus we find poor Lord Fermanagh, on 12 January 1712, wearily writing how relieved he was that Christmas was at last over: 'It has been a troublesome time, every day with the noise of either drums, trumpets, hautboys, pipes or fiddles, some days 400 guests, very few days under 100, so that, besides the vast expense, it has been very tiresome.'

Noël and Scarlett O'Aga

The O'Aga Family

Having decided to write a book about surviving and simplifying Christmas, which would at least help myself, I was then faced with the problem of research. Looking back through my diaries from 1971 to 1984, I found a distressing number of blank pages between the beginning of each December and the middle of each January, because Christmas itself always took over and I was too frantically busy or knackered to chronicle events.

Last year, whether exhausted, elated, drunk or sober, I made a point of writing my diary every night, right through December and into the New Year; and I hope that this book, drawn largely from these observations, will perhaps help people to avoid some of the pitfalls, or at least realise that their disasters are shared by others, and thus have a happier Christmas.

In the pages of this book you will meet a Christmas family. They consist of a housewife, Scarlett O'Aga, so called because she is always bustling about not very efficiently, saying she's 'got to get on', and has a shiny red face all Christmas from toiling over the Aga. Like many women, Scarlett is an Xmasochist, who only feels she is doing the festive season properly if she worries herself into the ground. Scarlett is married to Noël, so called because he is absolutely no-elp-at-all. Noël has a Scroogian attitude towards Christmas, a mistress called Ms Stress, and an undemanding job in the City, which he feels justifies his spending most of the festive season slumped in front of the telly, or boozing with his cronies in the Dog and Trumpet. Noël and Scarlett have two teenage children, Holly and Robin, two little ones, Carol and Nicholas, and a dog called Difficult Patch.

Finally, if this book appears a little jaundiced, I must apologise. It is simply that, having lived through Christmas 1985 from October to December, I then had to relive it all over again from January to March, as I wrote the book; and two Christmases in six months is rather too much.

Bisley, 1 April 1986

One: Christmas is Coming

Where are you going to spend Christmas this year?

'There was a point this Christmas,' said a girlfriend, 'as I was struggling to get the turkey out of the oven, and my husband was sweating away over the roast potatoes, when I asked myself for the hundredth time whether it was all worth it. The eager little faces all round the table – knife and fork at the ready in each tight little fist – were not those of the children but of the collection of geriatric grandparents, great aunts and uncles we seem to feed each year.'

The reason why so many couples resort to home fixtures – knackering as they may be – is that away fixtures are often infinitely worse. At least at home you can drink as much as you like, keep warm and not worry the whole time about your children breaking the place up.

At first sight this might not seem like a major issue; but the problem with Christmas – rather like having a baby – is that it occurs infrequently enough for us to be able each time to blot out the horrors of the previous one. Let me refresh your memory.

If you're newly married, or married without children, the Christmas fixtures row begins in October and goes as follows:

Wife: 'We're not going to your parents. No drink, paper napkins used twice, and plates whipped away before you've finished your last mouthful.'

Husband: 'We're not going to *your* parents. No central heating, no washing-up machine, and those bloody dogs.'

Whatever decision is taken, the row then continues until Twelfth Night.

The arrival of children in a marriage complicates things

even more. Away fixtures, unless grandparents live nearby and
are used to the children, can be an utter nightmare. If
Grandpapa puts his hand on his somewhat dicky heart, he
will admit how much he is dreading the visit; Granny is more
hypocritical.

'Such fun to have a houseful,' she flutes, upstaging her
bridge friends. 'All the grandchildren are descending.' (Rather
as though they were coming down in a spaceship. As a matter
of fact, if you don't see your grandchildren very often, they
can seem as alien as Martians.)

The day of the visit dawns. Suddenly there's the bang of
the Volvo door and three under-threes with frightful colds,
snot cascading in parallel lines from their nostrils, erupt into
the beautiful, ultra-tidy house, and start destroying the place
far more effectively than any bulldozer.

Grandpapa shouts a lot, because having so many people
around makes him nervous, and this unnerves the children even
more. Soon Ribena is spilt all over the new lemon-yellow sofa,
sticky fingers are edging towards the Rockingham, and at
lunchtime a precious glass (belonging to a complete set, given as
a wedding present forty years ago) is dropped and smashes on
the flagstones. Finally the Virgin Mary goes missing from the
crib, and, after the whole house has been up-ended and World
War III has broken out, is discovered under the spare-room bed
in the gross clasps of a lascivious Action Man.

Almost worse for grandparents than the helplessly permissive mother is the progressive daughter-in-law, the Après-
Spock health freak, who goes into orbit if poor Granny slips
little Carol a few Smarties between meals, or gives her Coke,
fried beefburgers and bubble-and-squeak for lunch. Then,
having been gratuitously beastly in conversation about the
Daily Telegraph, the progressive daughter-in-law proceeds to
whip out a long grey tit and breast-feed in the middle of a
Boxing Day drinks party.

And if the visiting mother gets uptight because her children
are behaving badly or being spoilt by Granny, her husband
will be soon complaining about his father-in-law. 'Mine's so
mean,' admitted one son-in-law. 'He not only waters the logs,
and keeps turning the light off outside the children's bedroom
at night, but, worst of all, he winces if I open another

bottle of wine from the two crates I've brought him.'

Even if you do take your own booze, you don't want to appear a soak in front of your in-laws. 'One year,' said a friend, 'we took up a crate of claret to my in-laws in Lancashire and, having polished it off, were asked to bury all the bottles in the garden, as my mother-in-law was so embarrassed by what the dustmen might think.'

On this subject I have never forgotten a hideously shameful occasion when my children were very young and my in-laws were staying. Having announced sanctimoniously, and untruthfully, that I never drink at home at lunchtime, I then laced my orange juice with gin to get me through the ordeal of grandparents' and children's lunch. My daughter, then aged two and a half, seized my glass, and, thinking it was straight orange juice, took a great swig. She swiftly spat it out all over her grandmother and declared that she'd been poisoned, whereupon Granny took a tiny sip, and recognised gin.

Some parents love and enjoy their grandchildren, and it seems sad that others only meet theirs at Christmas when everyone is at their most overwrought. One devoted grandmother said to me this year, 'We had Christmas for the first time in thirty-five years without children or grandchildren; absolute heaven, out to parties every day – result total exhaustion.'

Another equally devoted daughter-in-law told me: 'This year was the best Christmas I've had for sixteen years, because I finally plucked up courage to tell my extended family of in-laws and step-parents to get knotted, and that they couldn't all bum a free holiday off us. I hardened my heart, and in the process lightened it considerably.'

If you feel compelled to invite both your parents and your parents-in-law to spend Christmas with you, do consider asking them on alternate years or at least staggering the visits. This is because there is invariably rivalry between the two sides, caused by a very natural desire to be the most popular grandparents.

If there are two widowed grandmothers staying at the same time, the problem becomes even more acute and there's bound to be granny-mosity. There are also likely to be battles over who is the most helpful granny. A friend, faced with the unedifying sight of two grey-haired old ladies in dressing-gowns battling over the kettle early on Christmas morning, slipped a Valium in both their cups of coffee and had a very peaceful day.

If you're determined to stay with people other than relations at Christmas, do make a recce first. Their place may be ravishing in summer, sitting on the terrace, drinking Pimms with all the roses out, but winter can be a very different proposition.

A friend described Christmas in Yorkshire, 'where thermo-nuclear underwear was *de rigueur* to keep *rigor mortis* from setting in. As soon as dinner was announced, there would be an uncontrolled scramble upstairs by the in-house guests, ostensibly to wash their hands. Only when the lights on the Christmas tree dimmed to half their normal brightness did it click with our host that throughout the house every electric blanket was being turned on to Regulo Nine. The decanter of whisky in all the guest rooms (or gust rooms) was not just a sop for the sots; it was as essential as Kendal mint cake and a day-glo anorak is to a Lakeland climber, simply to propel one-self from the bedroom to the bathroom.'

Patrick Lichfield told me that when he was a child the butler always served Christmas dinner in an overcoat, and used to gauge the temperature by the icicle hanging from the chandelier. I'm sure that the upper classes have such a reputation for bed-hopping because vigorous sex was the only way you could keep warm in large country houses.

Finally, when it comes to the decision of where you're going to spend Christmas, let your head rule your heart. If you're weak-willed, from September onwards stick a large sign up by every telephone in the house which reads: 'WHAT A MARVEL-LOUS IDEA, BUT CAN I RING YOU BACK WHEN I'VE TALKED TO MY FAMILY/HUSBAND/MY LOVER/MY CAT?' and read that out to *every-one* who rings up about Christmas arrangements.

And curb the spirit of altruism. Before inviting another family to stay, spare a thought for your own poor children who may not enjoy having to entertain younger children or being patronised by older ones. The great mistake is to suddenly feel guilty and, after three vodka and tonics have given you the illusion that you have the patience of Job

coupled with the strength of Hercules, ring and invite your
entire extended family plus in-laws for a week. Keep invitations short: two or three days are quite long enough. Invite or
accept in the cold light of sobriety in front of your partner,
then you cannot be accused of pulling a fast one later.

Countdown

I can call spirits from the vasty deep freeze.

My most depressing and abiding Christmas memory is of
Bentalls of Kingston on Christmas Eve 1978, when a fat
woman charged the men's toiletries counter and having
bought ten bottles of Brut Aftershave, which were reduced
because of battered packaging, announced in satisfied tones
that that was all her menfolk's presents sewn up for Christmas
1979. Almost as frightful is the behaviour of eager beavers
who rush off to sales on 27 December to buy Christmas cards
and wrapping paper at half price for next year; or of the *Observer* Woman's Page who in December 1985 was telling its
readers the best place to order their 'corn-fed gobblers' for
Christmas 1986.

There is no doubt, on the other hand, that being prepared
is the secret of a more harmonious Christmas. If Joseph had
booked a room in advance, Jesus would not have been born in
a stable, and as most of us, like Mary and Joseph, are taxed
out of existence and very short of funds, it's better to spread
the cost of Christmas over a few months.

My own Christmas preparations start half-heartedly in late
August when I plant the indoor bulbs, in the faint hope that
they will bloom by Christmas and I won't have to fork out
fortunes in flowers in all the guests' bedrooms. Aware that it is
common to have different coloured bulbs in one bowl, I divide
them into neat little piles of one colour, only to have the dogs
chase one of the cats straight through the lot, muddling them
irretrievably so the bulbs emerge in tricolour – generally just
about in time for Easter. Do remember to keep the bulb fibre
bag, which has instructions printed on it telling you how far
the bulbs have to protrude before you remove them from their
dark hiding place.

From September onwards experts in the media will provide you with countdowns on Christmas activities:

> *Six weeks before Christmas:* make 550 tartlet cases and freeze (in our house you freeze anyway).
> *Five weeks before Christmas:* make 550 kiwi-fruit possets and freeze.
> *Four weeks before Christmas:* construct festive dinner-table centrepiece from gilded fir cones and milk-bottle tops and freeze.

Our hero, Noël, is so fed up with reading about Christmas preparations and listening to his wife Scarlett's endless recitation of tasks ahead that he fantasises wildly about a countdown à la Crippen:

> *Twenty days before Christmas:* mother-in-law pops in with Xmas gifts, batter her to death and freeze.
> *Ten days before Christmas:* father-in-law arrives in search of mother-in-law, batter him to death and freeze.
> *Seven days before Christmas:* Holly and Robin return from school and receive ditto treatment.
> *Two days before Christmas:* batter Scarlett, Nicholas, little Carol and Difficult Patch and freeze.
> *Christmas Eve:* buy one-way ticket to Rio.

I myself am not capable of a countdown routine. But the thing that saved us last year, when we had a continuous stream of people staying – most of them for several days – between Christmas Eve and 2 January, and we gave, in addition, a huge New Year's Day lunch party, was cooking in advance. This is elementary to most organised housewives, but it was the first year we'd had a proper deep-freeze. Consequently, we made a list of meals for those nine days, and spent the weekends leading up to Christmas cooking and freezing massive shepherd's pies, steak and kidney pies, fish pies, soups and oxtail stews. Unfortunately I kept sabotaging the plan by forgetting to tick things off as I took them out of the freezer.

There is absolutely no need, unless you find relaxation in

cooking, to make mince pies, sausage rolls, Christmas cake or Christmas pudding. Bought ones are just as good, particularly if you inject the latter two with brandy in the run-up to Christmas.

Never buy drink in advance because it's cheap: you just drink it in advance. For the same reason, hide boxes of chocolates.

Try not to waste time being over-elaborate. The December issue of one magazine had a ludicrous recipe for crackers made out of puff pastry stuffed with mincemeat, with cracker petticoats made of rice-paper rectangles trimmed with pinking shears. If you served those in our house, people would be so drunk that they'd try and pull them.

Remember that Christmas is not a culinary competition between mothers, daughters, sisters-in-law and (now that most men cook) sons-in-law as well. Women tend to behave as though they're taking a degree in Christmas and that the world will end if they get a third in sprouts, a fourth in bacon rolls, and fail bread sauce totally.

> *30 November:* don't forget to buy children Advent calendars and sparklers for Christmas dinner. Order logs and new cheque book.
> *9 December:* grouse shooting ends and Christmas grousing hots up.

Christmas presents

> *Spending beyond their income on gifts for Christmas –*
> *Swing doors and crowded lifts and draperied jungles –*
> *What shall we buy for our husbands and sons*
> *Different from last year?*
>
> Louis MacNeice

Every year it's the same. In about October, I'm nudged by telephone calls from female relations, asking, what would my children and husband like for Christmas?

'I don't know,' I wail helplessly, thinking that if I had any remotely good ideas, I'd keep them to myself. 'I expect they'd like money, but then wouldn't we all?'

Then, unable to face the horror of buying at least a hundred presents, I deliberately forget about shopping until the week before Christmas. As a result I spend three times as much as I ought, out of guilt and panic. There's nothing nice left in the shops. Everyone's using credit cards, so there's a half-hour wait, being goosed by other people's rolls of wrapping-paper, at every till. It's impossible to park because of euphemistically named Christmas pedestrianisation. Even in a town as civilised as Cirencester you need a helicopter. All the shop assistants are fed up, drunk and, in the men's shops, getting off with each other: 'You've got such a nice manner on the telephone, Mr Clissold.'

The Queen, according to the *News of the World*, buys 'stocking fillers like embroidered cushions and dainty boxes' from 'a discreet businessman' who calls every year at Buckingham Palace.

Last year, for the first time in my life, because I don't know any discreet businessmen and because I was writing a book about Christmas, I shopped early. The difference was wonderful and amazing. I bought most of my presents in Cheltenham, which as a stylish provincial town is hard to beat. Unlike London, all the shops you need are close together. I managed to polish off about fifty presents in one six-hour session.

Try and shop alone, then you can potter and move around without distraction. Leave the children with a girlfriend one day, and take her children, so that she can shop, on another. If you're working, a late-night shop opening early in December is far less harrowing or buffeting than lunch hours or Saturdays.

The next problem is what to buy. So many people spend so much money on useless presents – 'bath salts, and inexpensive scent', as John Betjeman put it, 'and hideous tie so kindly meant' – that it's a pity that grown-ups as well as children can't all write letters to Father Christmas in November listing what they want, which instead of vanishing up the chimney could be circulated to their relations.

One of the most skilled present-givers I know recommends shopping at home with a pencil, then going out and buying what you've written down and *nothing else*. The best presents, she claims, are always brainwork, and no one can think with aching feet.

A discreet businessman

The other school of present-giver makes a list of people who need presents, and goes off to the shops to seek inspiration.

'I start shopping in October with wild enthusiasm,' says my sister-in-law, 'rushing out and buying things I like the look of. The problem comes in the middle of December when I have to fit the presents to the recipient. It never works, and I end up with a pair of lacey teenage knickers for the 89-year-old man who used to dig the garden, and a Bach cantata tape for my father-in-law who is not only stone deaf, but hasn't got a tape recorder.'

The best presents are chosen with imagination, and convey the feeling that the giver has taken some trouble.

Another friend always tries to have a theme: one year she gave us all stunning mugs with our names on; another year she found old pine boxes of different shapes and sizes and had appropriate words and pictures painted on each one.

My husband, another inspired giver, digs out old sepia photographs of grandparents and great aunts on seaside donkeys or at picnics, and has them blown-up and framed for different members of the family. A good cheap idea is to find out the birth dates of everyone to whom you want to give a present, then mail the list to *The Times*, who send you back a Xerox of the front page of the paper on the day each person was born, wrapped like a scroll.

One Christmas my ex-housekeeper had the charming idea of giving me ten plates with photographs of all the family and each of the cats and dogs printed on them. Victorian name brooches are lovely too, but a bit hard to find if your name is Earl or Jody.

I also like double presents: a pretty vase filled with coffee-flavoured chocolate beans, or a Beatrix Potter box with a fiver inside, or presents that last, like a year's subscription to *Private Eye*, the *Spectator* or the *Tatler*. Not having young children any more, I find it very difficult imagining what my small godchildren would like. If you ask a shop assistant whether some toy would be suitable for a child of five, she always says yes.

For a child under a year, you don't have to buy them anything: just wrap up empty boxes – all they like is tearing at coloured paper.

Such is the power of the media that children usually want the toy most advertised on television. Last year it was the Transformer toy and My Little Pony. Prince William got the first and went one-up on the second, getting a real Shetland pony of his own. Prince Harry had to make do with Beatrix Potter pictures. When the permissive society was at its height, the most popular toy was a doll with a willy called Little Christopher; mercifully, most of the willies broke off in the post.

Children grow up so fast; do check how old they are. Remember the story of Jean Cocteau, who, when reproached by a female friend for neglecting his godchild, immediately dispatched a vast teddy bear.

'Was he thrilled?' he asked the mother when he bumped into her a week later.

'Not at all,' she said sourly, 'He's a colonel now.'

If you give clothes to the children of a working mother, try and get the sizes right, because she will never find the time to change them. Also, avoid giving them presents that have to be made up. Our attic upstairs groans with unused chemistry sets, untouched jigsaw puzzles, unassembled kits and model aeroplanes, and corn dollies that were never made. (Perhaps the latter should have got together with Little Christopher.)

Try not to over-buy. As a mother at Christmas, particularly if you're working, you may feel riddled with guilt because you have not been spending enough time with your children, and consequently bankrupt yourself on extra and expensive presents. You have only to look at the sea of over-priced plastic, strewn unplayed-with over the nursery floor on Boxing Day, to realise that you have over-reacted.

It's hard to find the perfect presents for teenagers, because they usually want paraphernalia to attract the opposite sex, and, as teenage fashions change with the speed of light, anything a centimetre too short or too long will be chucked out. My poor daughter got fifteen pairs of legwarmers the year before last and never wore any because they were no longer fashionable.

You're usually safe with record tokens and Way In or Miss Selfridge gift tokens. Another very good present, if teenagers are into parties, is a voucher to hire a ball dress for the night from One Night Stand at 44 Pimlico Road, London. Vast, dark, baggy jerseys are popular with both sexes. Don't do what I did last year, which was to buy wildly fashionable jewellery, tights and jerseys for all my nieces and teenage goddaughters and then be quite unable to resist wearing them myself. I then had to go out and buy a whole lot more presents.

Teenage boys always push their luck, like Adrian Mole asking his mother, who was on social security, for a word processor, a portable colour television or an electric typewriter. Similarly, last year my son suggested I give him a hi-fi or a shot gun; and when I bleated that I couldn't afford it, he replied with perfect logic that I could have, if I hadn't spent my time during the past year pouring drink down other people's throats.

You can be sure that any good suggestions for teenage boys featured in the paper – the key-ring that whistled back at you when you whistled for it, the alarm clock that stopped bleeping when you shouted at it, but bleeped again five minutes later and carried on until you got up – will be sold out when you get to the shop, so telephone first to check.

Men are almost more difficult than teenage boys. Having no colour sense, and being blonde and blue-eyed, with a dark-haired, dark-eyed husband, I tend to rush up to terrified dark-eyed, dark-haired shop assistants thrusting purple shirts dripping with pins against their bosoms, with one eye closed (so they think I'm winking) saying, 'Does this colour suit you?' They always say yes.

Men, who probably long to be given Samantha Fox in a grass skirt and a lawn mower, tend to get black silk pyjamas as the ultimate in sophistication. Invariably they also get something to do with drink: bottle-openers, glasses, wine-coolers. Noël would prefer a wife-cooler over Christmas. A friend says that one of her uncles got fourteen bottles of various kinds of booze one year, and nothing else. He was terribly upset because, he said, anyone would think he was an alcoholic – which in fact he was.

Last year it was the boxer rebellion. Every man chucked out his Y-fronts, and was given boxer shorts, the male equivalent of French knickers. Some were covered in pigs, others in lipstick marks or Father Christmases. 'So erotic,' one woman told the *Standard*, 'thinking of all that frivolity under his dark grey city suit.' Turnbull and Asser were offering silk boxer shorts at £25 and, rather tweely, striped shirts and matching shorts; better than transparent boxer shorts, which make a man look like one of those cellophane packs of giblets in the supermarket.

Sadly, one tends to get into a rut with presents. My husband has always said that he loves the shirts I give him. It was only after twenty-four years of marriage, as we walked down Jermyn Street, that he actually admitted that he preferred much shorter collars.

One man got so fed up with his wife's ghastly taste in shirts that he took her out to lunch in Jermyn Street. Next door was a man's clothes shop, where the husband had primed the shop assistants to place two shirts that he liked in the front of the window. As he and his wife walked past, he pointed them out, telling her how much he adored them. Sadly she got so plastered at lunch that she rushed back afterwards and bought the wrong shirts.

Men always claim that women are hard to give presents to. I'm dead easy – all I want is cashmere jerseys, in any colours except red, orange, maroon, fuschia pink and custard yellow; silk shirts in ditto; jewellery; records; books; scent; gardening tokens and the man who plays Jeff Colby in *Dynasty*.

One friend, whose husband is absolutely hopeless at shopping, makes a point of going round several of her favourite shops, and making a list for him – rather like a wedding list. That way he feels as though he's chosen the present, and she gets what she wants. The only shop he baulked at was Ann Summers, where her list included a vibrator. He claimed that the competition would be too awesome, and he couldn't bear the bedroom sounding like a building site.

It's easier, of course, if your husband's very rich, like the woman interviewed on television by Clive James who lived in Dallas, who was dickering between choosing a $55,000 and a $65,000 diamond bracelet as her Christmas present. One of the best-looking men I ever met always took his wife to the place in the world of her choice as a Christmas present. Sadly, after they had driven across the desert from Tangier to Northern Nigeria one Christmas, the vehicle broke up, and so did the marriage.

First prize for initiative goes to the little girl who, having spent all her Christmas present money on sweets, calmly removed an unopened pair of tights from her mother's chest of drawers, wrapped it up and gave it back to her for Christmas.

First prize for the romantic gesture goes to the lover whose girlfriend wanted a birdbath. When she came down on Christmas morning, and drew back the kitchen curtains, she found the most beautiful stone birdbath, wrapped in gold tinsel. Over it hung a banner saying, 'HAPPY CHRISTMAS MY DARLING,' in huge letters.

It's no good trying to improve people at Christmas. In the fifties, Tim Jaques gave his father a book on Picasso, hoping it would initiate him into the joys of modern art. His father merely yelled 'Filth' and hurled the book across the room.

Bestsellers are also hazardous presents. Many years ago my brother and I each gave the other a copy of *Doctor Zhivago*. Be careful, too, if you're going to read the book before giving it, not to turn down the pages or drop it in the bath, and re-member that if you do cut off the price, because it's considered bad form not to do so, the recipient can't then change it.

Some people choose presents deliberately calculated to irritate. Mothers pointedly give socks and underpants to their married sons, because 'someone's got to look after you, dar-ling', and the WVS cook-book to their daughters-in-law be-cause 'any child could follow the recipes'. Or you could send a *Spare Rib* calendar, which has a special menstrual table for charting your periods, to a moody sister-in-law; and *Karate for Beginners* to her battered husband. Then there's always the remaindered copy of the *Jane Fonda Workout Book* for Rich Great Aunt Phyllis in the hope of pushing her into an early coronary.

A divorced friend claims that he realised that his marriage was coming to an end when his millionaire mother-in-law gave him a bottle of corked red wine for Christmas, and his three-year-old daughter a jumping furry toy which was on discount at $1 at the local supermarket. Even more poignant is the story of the wife who, a few years ago when video machines were really expensive, saved all year out of the housekeeping to buy one for her husband, and in return only got a grapefruit knife and two peach satin-padded coat hangers. That mar-riage also broke up shortly afterwards.

But with the best will in the world we all have our disasters. My ex-housekeeper once gave her eighty-year-old mother a frantically expensive footwarmer into which you put both feet like a muff. Unfortunately her mother kept forgetting she'd got it on, leaping to her feet to answer the door or the telephone, and falling flat on her face.

Beware, too, the joke present. Last year one girlfriend gave her husband a box of sweets with contraceptives inside them. Somehow the presents got muddled up, and her newly-widowed mother-in-law opened them by mistake.

'I watched, frozen with horror, as she unwrapped one and popped it in her mouth. Her eyes began to roll slightly as she chewed helplessly on the rubber. She was a terrific sport, though, as she pulled it from her mouth, she said, "Well really, my dears, I'm about the only person in this room who has absolutely *no* use for this at all." '

Another friend committed an even worse howler one year when, knowing that his terribly straight-laced mother was a fan of Peter Cook and Dudley Moore, he bought her the famous 'Derek and Clive' record. Not having heard the record himself, he had no idea what was on it. Imagine the ghastly silence as they all sat down to listen to it after lunch and a stream of four-letter words, obscenities and general sexual depravity poured out. The friend was so embarrassed that he left home that afternoon.

Be careful of giving back presents you've been given to the original donor. If by some hideous chance you do, the only solution is to say airily: 'People always give presents they want themselves, so I thought I'd get one for you this year.'

Finally, there's always the present whose function you can't identify. One of our house guests this year was given by the Turkish lady who runs her local off-licence a 2 ft by 3 ft strip of knitted wool in chilblain mauve, which tapered into long ties at each end. After much hysterical speculation, we all decided that it must be a bottom bra for the pear-shaped figure.

Don't forget to budget for Christmas boxes for the paper boy, the dustmen, the milkman and the postman: they jolly well deserve it, particularly in the country. If you can't afford to tip the dustmen, you should instantly move to an area like Lambeth, with a left council that doesn't approve of such capitalist tokens of appreciation.

Christmas at work

Gordon Selfridge used to give all his staff a plum pudding and a pep pill at Christmas, presumably because he realised the pressures they would be under.

Commuting, in particular, in the run-up to Christmas is absolute murder, with cars and buses at a standstill, and all the tubes and trains crowded out because everyone's pouring into the big cities to shop or see the lights. On the way home from a hard day's work you are liable to find everyone either festively drunk, or helping someone else to be sick.

It's very difficult to operate efficiently at work if you have a raging hangover. When the Managing Director makes his rounds, ring up Dial-a-disc and, as he passes through your office, say: 'Excellent – you'll be clinching the deal in a few days will you, sir?' and the MD will pass on, confident that you're successfully occupied.

Then there's the office party – the season of which begins in December. During it, people will drink far too much, lunge at one another, tell the Managing Director he's a twerp and pour the office vegan's sprout wine down the word processor to cackles of mirth.

Despite Mr Tebbit's 'Clean Up Britain' campaign, there was absolutely no evidence that anyone behaved any better at office parties last year. At the Imperial War Museum, as early as 1 December, a couple were surprised copulating in a tank, and by 3 December a friend had been caught *in flagrante* on the office snooker table with one of the typing pool. The Managing Director who caught them wasn't at all upset by the sexual transgression – merely outraged that they might be ripping the cloth.

How you behave at office parties, however, should depend on how much you value your job. There's an unwritten law that no one actually gets booted out for a misdemeanour. But the transgressor will no longer be regarded as officer material, and will probably be kicked out on some trumped-up excuse in the New Year. Such a pity one can't behave gloriously badly and Tippex the whole incident out afterwards.

But with fines for sexual harassment up to £500 these days, how do susceptible males stay out of trouble at the office party?

One friend suggests that offices should introduce tube straps from the ceiling. Thus you could remain vertical, however much you knocked back, but with one hand in the strap and the other clutching your glass, both would be kept out of mischief. Or you could send every senior married man a Sarah-Keays-o-gram, in which a virago in a smock would burst through the door and warn him of the dire consequences of tangling with one's secretary.

If men are determined to scuffle behind the filing cabinets, there are a few rules for cutting down the hassle when they get home. Wear a red shirt, so that the lipstick doesn't show up. Avoid girls with frosted make-up – glitter clings to your cheek worse than burrs on a Persian cat. And slip an air-freshener disc into your breast pocket to neutralise the cheap scent.

In my experience, as this is the one night when the most junior typist can have a crack at the Managing Director, most of the sexual harassment comes from women. One good-looking boss was grumbling that at his office party last year a secretary asked him to hold her drink for her. The moment he had glasses in both hands, she promptly unzipped his flies, to whoops of joy all round.

And some women, at least, don't seem to mind a liberty being taken if it's civil enough. A peer I know, whose marriage is going through a sticky patch, promised his wife to be home from the office by ten o'clock. During the evening he was hotly pursued by a comely switchboard girl and was drunk enough to offer her a lift home. He pulled into a lay-by and, aware that time was fast running out, slid a hand under her skirt.

Whereupon she said in outraged tones: ' 'Ere! D'you fink I'm common or somefink? Tits first, please.'

Some firms hold their bashes in restaurants. You see those rings of self-conscious conviviality in the middle of some trattoria, the whole department in paper hats, eating turkey and silicone chipolatas, the sales manager flushed under a purple fore and aft: 'We'll stick to the cha'eau-bo'led, Luigi, the Spanish one.'

One respected television programme has such disruptive office orgies that they've been banned from every restaurant in the West End, and last year settled for some unwary Indian restaurant in Twickenham.

'You don't need directions to get to our parties,' explained the floor manager, 'You just follow the blue flashing light.'

The Kantara Taverna in Shaftesbury Avenue is so popular that it's always booked solid throughout December. One of the incentives is that parties of more than fifteen get a belly dancer thrown in free. Watching her shimmering through the tables trying to galvanise a party from Barclays Bank, I noticed a sinister new development. Every time she pressed her juddering midriff against the flushed face of a department head, or persuaded some glassy-eyed cashier to roll his shirt above the nipples and dance with her, the entire typing pool leapt whooping to their feet, and, whipping out those matchbox cameras, snapped the compromising moment for posterity.

Even worse is the Christmas drink in the pub with secretaries smoking cigarettes at right angles, and lifting their thighs off bar stools to make them look thinner. Every so often one of them teeters across to order: 'One Cointreau and lemon for Charlene, a Malibu and Coke for Tracey, a snowball for Carole, two light and bitters for Ray and Terry, a pineapple juice for Mr Patel; come on, Pauline, you're one behind – try a Pernod and Cassis this time.' Afterwards everyone is sick – it's a pity that the Tories don't start their clean-up campaign by erecting a few vomitoriums round the West End. The most intelligent garment for a girl to wear to an office party is a wet suit.

But finally, as you embark on the assault course of the office party season, spare a thought for the poor wife at home, who's usually banned from office parties because she inhibits the fun even more than the MD. No wonder she gets a shade beady, as she copes not only with the Christmas run-up and the first riotous days of the school holidays, but also with her husband staggering home late and plastered night after night.

I am reminded of the touching story of a beautiful friend of mine, who'd just fallen asleep after midnight, when her husband returned tight from the office party with his equally drunk boss and the boss's secretary. Dutifully, my beautiful friend got up, made black coffee and beds in separate rooms for the boss and his secretary, as neither was fit to drive, and collapsed back into bed again. Waking at five, she found no husband beside her, and set out to find him – no luck downstairs. Coming back up, she heard a giggle from the spareroom. Seeing the light on and the door ajar, she tiptoed forward, heart thumping unpleasantly. Recognising her husband's back, she gave a wail of anguish; whereupon the back swung round in horror, turning out to belong to the boss.

Having solved one problem, she set out to find her husband. She finally located him, fast asleep in the nursery. Not wanting to wake her, he had curled up under the duvet with his three-year-old daughter.

Next evening he came home with an early Christmas present from the boss – the biggest box of Black Magic she had ever seen.

Christmas cards

One of the saddest stories I ever heard was of an old-age pensioner called Annie, who was taken ill at Christmas. When the ambulance men came to take her to hospital they found one solitary card on her mantelpiece which said, 'To Annie with love from Annie'.

For this reason, I tend to send cards only to people who are old, poor or lonely, and might not get many. Less admirably, I also send them to those who may advance my career. My cards usually go off at the last minute and arrive in time to wish everyone a happy New Year; or else they don't make it at all and lie around on the hall table for weeks with names but no addresses, because the relevant telephone book has gone AWOL.

After Christmas I go through the incoming pile, crying 'Oh how sweet', and vowing to answer the letters inside – but somehow I never do.

In 1984, when I was finishing a book, I didn't send any cards at all. Perhaps I should have advertised the fact in the personal column of *The Times*, but I knew I would have bankrupted myself afterwards ringing all my friends to check if they'd seen the ad. Instead, my husband ran me off a hundred letters in the office, to send out in the New Year, apologising for not sending cards and hoping to see the people soon. Shamingly, I found the pile untouched under a potted plant in my study last November.

There is a theory that if you post your Christmas cards early, you not only spend less because you can use a second-class stamp, but also you get more cards back. I'm not sure that this is true. Often when you get a card, telling you that some long-lost mate is alive, well and still loves you, you don't feel the same compulsion to send them one back.

I also notice that the number of cards we get doesn't alter, whether we send any or not. I always feel riddled with guilt if I don't send someone a card, but it's awfully arrogant to assume that anyone will notice its lack among all the cards they get.

It's a good thing that Gallup hasn't conducted a poll as to how many cards the average person receives, or we'd all be as neurotic about slipping below the national average as we are about sex.

To swell the numbers, lots of people bring out last year's cards; or leave the haul from a November birthday at the back; or bring cards back from the office at weekends; or take home-ones in to the office during the week. And they always put the important ones from Margaret and Denis, or Neil and Glenys, at the front. Lord Hailsham still had one from Charles and Di up in August.

My husband and I usually have to translate cards for each other:

'Who the hell's that?' he says.

'Oh, some man who wrote to me about badger baiting,' I say, 'And who the hell's that?'

'Oh, some girl I helped get a job in publishing.'

We always have at least ten cards from unidentified people called John. Then you get reproachful cards from the mothers of neglected godchildren: 'Isabella's nearly eighteen now, you know.' Childless couples often add their dog's name to the card.

If people don't know your husband's name, they put, 'To you both'; or your children's names, 'To you all'. If you can't remember people's surnames, put, 'To all at the Old Rectory', on the envelope.

Cards are often trying to tell you something. Couples who send you photographs of themselves surrounded by all their children are saying that a very sticky patch in their marriage has been circumnavigated. A husband who has walked out on his wife often sends you a photograph of himself surrounded by his laughing children, which can be translated as, 'You may think I was fiendish to Samantha, but the children don't.' Then there is the card from an ex-mother-in-law deliberately forgetting to include the new wife or calling her by the wrong name, which can trigger off a row well into the New Year.

The artistic or the impoverished tend to paint their own cards. It never hurts to send a card to one's creditors, although when an artist friend painted the most exquisite card for his bank manager, signing it with his bank account number to illustrate how brilliantly witty and potentially able to make money he was, it didn't stop the bank manager bouncing all his cheques in the New Year.

I can never understand the mentality of people who hang their cards on clothes lines across the room. Not only do they act as a dangerous garotte-a-gran, if some ancient relation wanders in to find her specs at night and the light by the door doesn't turn on; but also if you put cards on the furniture it's a blissful excuse not to dust for a month. The same goes for cards pinned to the back of an open-planned staircase, or attached by spangled clothes pegs to shiny ribbons (Tesco's idea).

Prince Andrew uses his own photographs of Windsor Castle as Christmas cards. His card, we are told, takes pride of place on the old clothes horse used by the Queen to display her favourite cards.

Today a large percentage of Christmas cards are sold to raise money for charity, which, while good for those in need, is generally lousy for artistic standards. In the old days, when there was only the occasional insipid offering painted by the mouth or by the feet, we always saved our prettiest Christmas cards in the hope of one day sticking them on a screen; but few in recent years have been worth keeping.

But it's interesting how the old themes recur.

'You put up too many cards again!'

Here are our top ten most popular subjects in 1970 compared with 1985:

1970

Festive robins	20
Mufflered snowmen	19
Regimental crests	17
Cottage with light in snowy dell	16
Blessed virgins	14
Jolly cardinals drinking indifferent claret by roaring fire	12
Old masters	10
Puffed-cheek Dickensian trumpeters	9
Santa and his reindeer crew (usually all pissed)	8
Pheasants in flaming bracken	5

1985

Santa and his reindeer crew (all sober because of drink-drive laws)	20
Old masters	19
Cottage with light in snowy dell	17
Blessed virgins	16
Pheasants or game birds in snow	16
Simpering bug-eyed mufflered tots in snow	16
Festive robins	8
Mufflered mice	8
Lovable mongrels	7
London street scenes	5
Puffed-cheeked Dickensian trumpeters	1

Relegated to the Second Division

Regimental crests (because of post-Falklands disillusionment?) ONLY	1
Jolly cardinals (Paisley rules OK?)	0

Carols

'My God,' said a secretary, wandering along Oxford Street, and seeing a crib in a department store window, 'they're even trying to bring religion into Christmas these days.'

In the ghastly commercialism and hair-tearing of the
run-up to Christmas it is only too easy to forget that we
are celebrating the birth of Christ and its message of
goodwill towards men. Take a look at our attitude to carol
singers.

The Oxford Book of Carols is full of descriptions of learned
doctors being delightedly woken up at six in the morning by
the sweet singing of mill girls, or of the squire expansively
opening his door and inviting all the carol singers inside to
enjoy mince pies and wassail.

Today, terrified of contact and extortion, Scarlett says, 'Oh
bugger, carol singers,' and, upending the housekeeping jar,
wonders if she's being stingy only offering them 20p, and
usually settles for 50p. She thinks it was grossly unfair that
poor Joan Collins was attacked in the *Daily Mail* the other day
for only giving some carol singers a fiver.

It seems sad that the pleasure we ought to feel when people
sing us carols is ruined by irritation at being blackmailed into
giving them money, and embarrassment that they are singing
directly at us.

But it was the same in the twenties when Laurie Lee was
young: 'Mile after mile we went,' he writes in *Cider with Rosie*,
'fighting against the wind, falling into snowdrifts, and navi-
gating by the lights of the house. And yet we never saw our
audience. We called at house after house, we sang in court-
yards and porches outside windows ... we received nuts,
cakes, figs, preserved ginger, cough drops and money, but we
never once saw our patrons. We sang as it were at the castle
walls.' Extraordinary, as Godfrey Smith pointed out in his
book *The Christmas Reader*, that no one ever came out to see
the boys or to wish them a Happy Christmas.

Moved by reading this and now living only a couple of
miles away from Laurie Lee's valley, I vowed that things
would be different this year. Wassail was beyond me, but I
bought in several packets of mince pies, to offer to any visiting
carol singers. Alas, none came.

Things were very different when we lived in London. In
Putney we were bombarded by scruffy schoolboys trampling
on the flower beds and yelling 'Li'el donkey, li'el donkey,' or
fat teenagers croaking out, 'We wish you a merry Christmas',

'They don't *look* like carol singers!'

to the accompaniment of stifled giggles, then forgetting the words.

One year, after paying out to five lots of singers in an evening, we heard the strains of ' 'Ark the 'Erald,' with no one hitting the top E, yet again, and I rushed to the door to tell them to go forth and multiply in rather more explicit terms, and found the rosy-cheeked face of the vicar's wife, shining above a row of little children.

In 1981, because my husband and I had gone to bed and took a long time to answer the door, I caught some carol singers writing four-letter words in the snow on the top of our car. Rather sheepishly they started singing another carol. Having given them 20p, I was about to go in when a woman in a folk-weave skirt said very huffily, 'We are collecting for Cambodia, not for ourselves you know.'

Nativity plays

> *When Mary heard she was to be the mother of Jesus she went and sang the Magna Carta.*
> Schoolboy Common Entrance essay

Christmas approaches. Realising that the children will soon be breaking up, Scarlett O'Aga steps up her panicking. Buckling under Christmas shopping, she staggers past boutiques pounding out sexy pop music, and wishes that she had a salary to blue on party glitter and was at an office party being propositioned.

Meanwhile at the office, the harassed working wife is tearing her hair. She has lost the roneoed letter about mince pies for the PTA Christmas knees-up; she's already forgotten to make paper-chains for the children's formrooms and to provide a pot of jam for the school Christmas Fayre (she wishes teachers would learn to spell); nor did she have time to wash her daughter's angel dress between performances of the nativity play. She still has to pack up a bottle of wine and a herbal cushion as end-of-term presents for her children's respective form mistresses, although from the amount of time she'd had to take off work to look after her own children during the teacher's strike, she feels they ought to be giving *her* presents.

Finally, even though she hasn't done any Christmas shopping yet, she is trying to screw up courage to ask her boss for yet another afternoon off, this time to attend her son's nativity play.

If she does get permission, she must turn up early to get a seat. So many children come from broken homes these days that nativity plays are packed out with both mothers and fathers turning up with new partners, and several new children.

One headmistress, anxious to fill the hall on the night, urged all the children to bring their parents, whereupon a small boy shot up his hand and asked: 'How many parents may one bring?'

Nativity plays are hazardous affairs. The standard of acting is abysmal, the singing even worse; the curtain collapses; Joseph is always playing Jacks with the oxen or punching the shepherds when he should be making his entrance, the heavenly host either burst into tears or wave like mad when they locate their parents in the audience; the Virgin Mary's front teeth are missing; and the innkeeper assures her that there's buckets of room at the inn if she and Joseph are prepared to share a bathroom. But it doesn't matter, even if the angel drips hot candle wax on the ass or the star fuses, because to the mothers and fathers their own child is the only star and its performance is bound to move them to tears.

Often the Virgin Mary's parents are separated and acrimonious, and kick off by firmly sitting at opposite ends of the same gym bench, but are forced next to one another by lack of space. Drying each other's tears afterwards, they often end up in the pub together.

Nativity plays tend to be very sophisticated these days, with children miming to taped songs from *Godspell* and *Jesus Christ Superstar*, and some father, who's a BBC cameraman, videoing all the tears and cock-ups for posterity.

Until a few years ago, all the children wanted to be Mary or at least the Angel Gabriel. Today, I am told, the most sought after part is Herod.

Two: Bearing Gifts
We Traverse Too Far

The Lovelorn

Christmas, with all its loving-kindness, togetherness and compulsory good will, is the worst possible time to be unhappy in love. It's a nightmare on your own, but even in the bosom of your family it's a pretty lethal brand of loneliness if there's no special man to love you.

Perhaps pre-Christmas parties – traditionally the hunting season of the unattached – will yield something. But it's always a strain going to parties on your own, worrying whether you can afford a taxi, or if you'll be able to find your way if you go by bus. Will you find a parking space if you take your car, and if you do, will you be able to have enough to drink to conquer your shyness, but not so much that you're done for drunk-driving? If you take a man whom you don't fancy for moral support, will you be able to get rid of him, if you meet someone you do?

If you really feel shy, offer to take round a bottle, or a plate of canapés. Candida Crewe, who once wrote a marvellous piece for the *Evening Standard* on parties and the single girl, suggested that if you get really desperate you should imagine all the people at the party in the nude, which will make you laugh and look attractive.

If you do fancy a man, one of the simplest ways of telling him so is to send him a Christmas card, and put 'lots of love from' inside. It's less overt than a valentine card, and much cheaper than giving a party so that you can issue him with a casual invitation.

At Christmas, you will often find that even current admirers seem to be going off the boil. This is because everyone's so frantically busy that people tend – unless they're besottedly in love – to neglect even those they are very fond of. The answer is to hang in and don't make scenes – everyone else will. Your beloved may temporarily have succumbed to some Jezebel at an office party, or be too broke to take you out, but he'll probably be back in the New Year.

There's such a shortage of glamorous spare men these days that it's a pity that an unattached girl can't hang up a pair of green gumboots, and find them filled on Christmas morning by a handsome heterosexual single farmer, waiting to whisk her off to some tax haven. If all else fails she can always put out a bucket to catch the drips in the hall.

Adultery

The days dividing lover and lover.

Another horror is not being able to spend Christmas with your lover because he or she is married to someone else. One sees all those couples embracing frantically in telephone booths near Simpson's of Piccadilly, or sobbing drunkenly on each other's necks outside Fortnum's.

'Only nine days till 2 January, Noël darling,' cries Ms Stress: 'You'd better hang on to the bracelet, darling. Gordon's bound to suspect something if I take it home. Promise to ring on Christmas Day: if Gordon's in the room, I'll pretend you're a wrong number.'

Then Ms Stress vanishes into a taxi, and is embarrassingly only five yards away an hour later because the traffic's so frightful.

'There is no doubt,' admitted one girlfriend, 'that my adulterous Christmases were the worst in my whole life, because I was single and he was going back to his wife. Christmas Eve was spent plodding from one West End shop to another, tears pouring down my face, as "Oh Come All Ye Faithful" pealed out over Oxford Street.'

'The unhappiness and sense of rejection of those Christmases when I was divorced,' wrote another woman friend, 'is something I would never wish to live through again.'

'The very mention of "Christmas" would plunge me into

despair. I had fallen passionately in love with a married man, which made things even worse. I remember so vividly those nights sitting at home alone knowing that my lover, and, as I thought, the whole world and his wife, were out at pre-Christmas parties. The brooding, pining and imagining would get out of all proportion.

'I sat over the telephone willing it to ring, and when it didn't, I'd go and have a bath, and if it still didn't, I'd have another, then it would ring and, mad with excitement, I'd rush to answer it; only to find it was a girlfriend, who'd been at the same party as my lover, and kindly thought I'd like to know he was fine, a bit drunk but in dazzling form. That was all I needed. How could he? Back to the bath, not only to drown my sorrows but wanting to drown myself.'

As well as loneliness, adultery at Christmas is fraught with hazards because lovers, primed by drink and a feeling that the world is going to end anyway, get much more reckless than usual. One barrister I know was having a Christmas Eve bunk-up with his mistress in his flat in Belgravia, when the front door opened and in marched his mother-in-law, who'd been sent a spare key to deliver the Christmas presents.

Another friend was driving down to the country cottage together with his wife and children and a boot crammed with Christmas Fayre, when the mistress, drunk from the office party, rang up on the car telephone and her tearfully amorous declaration was heard by all.

If a lover gets desperate and rings home at a sticky moment, it is far too lame an excuse to pretend that he's a wrong number. Say it's an obscene telephone call, let it run for five seconds and then slam down the telephone; the disgusting things the caller is alleged to have said should explain your blushes.

Husbands who don't want to get rumbled shouldn't leave Christmas present bills lying around. Scarlett thinks it very odd that a Janet Reger négligé Noël bought for her appears to have got lost in the post. It also seems odd that Noël, having allegedly spent six hours at the office party, returns home at midnight perfectly sober.

Noël, on the other hand, should watch out, if Scarlett suddenly starts buying pink, six-foot, fluffy teddy bears

'It's either a pash on the organist
or too much communion wine!'

allegedly for herself just before Christmas, or a Janet Reger négligé because she thought it suited her, or, even more sinister, a yearning pop record, on the excuse that she heard it on Radio One and liked the words. Equally, if Scarlett keeps running round the corner to visit some boring girlfriend, she's either using the boring friend's telephone, picking up letters, or admiring the dozen red roses, or the parrot that's being looked after for her. If she suddenly starts looking wonderful over Christmas, and doesn't put on at least seven pounds misery-eating – the marriage is in trouble.

The newly separated

The first Christmas after a marriage break-up tends to be murder.

'I was on my own,' said one girlfriend, 'I couldn't sleep, and I got up on Christmas morning as soon as it was light, and took the dog for a long, long walk; no one was about and I felt as though I was the last person left in the world.'

'My first Christmas after my husband walked out was just all right,' said another friend, 'because both the children came home, and my parents-in-law insisted on coming to stay with me, because they said they loved me, and were so sorry about the whole thing.' (Probably also because she's the most brilliant cook.)

Another friend, left by her lover after seven years, spent Christmas week totally alone.

'I read, I slept, I drank, I cried a lot, I didn't eat a thing, and I felt worse than I've ever felt, particularly because my family kept ringing up from Spain to see if I was still alive. But after Christmas I felt great, and as though I'd grown up, because I'd survived.'

Allowances should be made for the newly separated, particularly the woman, who ask you round for drinks because they can't stand the loneliness and then cancel at the last moment because they can't face the togetherness. They also tend to ring you on Boxing Day, saying that they might drop in, so you stay in all day. They never turn up. Later you find that they have done the same to six other people, needing the reassurance that they could go somewhere if they wanted to.

Newly separated men survive better, because there's such a dearth of spare males, and because of a quite mistaken belief that men can't survive for a moment on their own. Their insecurity manifests itself in a different way. At every party they're asked to, they turn up with a different, usually uninvited, girl so that they needn't undergo the humiliation of arriving or leaving on their own.

The boyfriend

One of the great traumas for parents – particularly mothers – is the first time one of the children announces he's going to spend Christmas at his girlfriend's parents. You realise that you're no longer indispensable. Comfort yourself that it's probably even more traumatic for the girlfriend's parents, who may well be meeting a future son-in-law for the first time, and are worried stiff about how they'll all get on.

Sleeping arrangements, for example, cause a lot of headaches. A friend told me how her beautiful twenty-year-old daughter rolled up one year with an ageing satyr with brushed-forward grey curls.

'He was at least five years older than me,' she said. 'When he asked where he was sleeping, I tried to be very modern and said I'd put them both in Henry's dressing-room. Whereupon he looked dreadfully shocked and said there was nothing like *that* between them, so I had to rush off and iron yet another pair of sheets and make up another bed. The ridiculous thing was that they commuted all night between the two bedrooms. I suppose that, regarding us as potential in-laws, he wanted to appear respectable. He wrecked his prospects when Henry wandered absent-mindedly into his dressing-room to get some cufflinks and found the satyr blow-drying his grey curls.'

On the other hand, if you firmly put the couple in different rooms from the start, you may be accused of being stuffy. Another friend said that her husband always used to soften this approach by warning the young man, with a slight wink, to be careful because the floorboards in the landing passages creaked like mad.

The visiting suitor, on the other hand, should find out in advance whether the family change for Christmas dinner if he thinks that there's any risk that they may. Then he can bring a dinner jacket if necessary. He should avoid getting so drunk at the office party that he arrives four hours late for dinner on Christmas Eve, or, even worse, doesn't make it until next morning. He should bring lots of presents for all the family, say how pretty the house is looking, and how pretty his hostess is, when his host is out of the room. He should be appreciative about the food, and never help himself to drinks.

Similarly, girls meeting possible in-laws for the first time should avoid flirting with the father too much. Too much make-up during the day and violently dyed hair is inadvisable in both sexes.

Be very nice to the family dog. One young man scuppered his chances of marrying a very rich girl one Christmas Eve. Having been left in the drawing-room with the house Chihuahua, which repeatedly mounted his leg, he finally gave a vicious kick, and the dog performed a perfect parabola, passing his hostess at eye-level as she entered the room.

Don't get up too early: around ten o'clock is perfect, which will give the hostess time to digest her Alka-seltzer, straighten the kitchen and get the dog hairs off the sofa. Midday is much too late, particularly if the suitor then slopes off to the pub and comes back belligerent and late for lunch, and starts being horrid about Mrs Thatcher.

A friend described the tragedy of the perfectly organised Christmas lunch being sabotaged by late arrivals:

'At twelve o'clock, all the family had arrived except my daughter, Priscilla, and some chap she had invited for Christmas. Champagne and happy exchange of presents followed, but no Priscilla. We waited an hour, then the telephone rang: Priscilla and boyfriend were still at some party but definitely on their way. I felt very uptight. Waited another hour, still no Priscilla. Dish up, no Priscilla, everyone now hopping mad. Just as we started to eat, Priscilla and friend swept in, radiant with seasonal "spirits", to an icy reception.

'Then, horrors, the turkey tasted decidely off. I decided to keep quiet.

' "Is it goose?" asked Priscilla.

' "Tastes like pheasant," said the boyfriend, putting his knife and fork together.

'Not another mouthful could I face, I fled to the loo and sobbed my heart out.'

The visiting boyfriend should try and be helpful, loading the washing-up machine or bringing in logs; but not to the extent of one young suitor in Ireland who set fire to the house by lighting the sitting-room fire with a can of petrol. Dispensing winter fuel can be carried too far.

The stepchild

One of the worst casualties at Christmas can be the stepchild. When the marriage first breaks up, he does rather well. Each parent battles to have him for Christmas, and all the relations are so worried that he may be traumatised by the break-up that he is showered with presents and love.

I remember when my daughter was eight she came home one day purple with rage because her best friend, whose father had just walked out, was getting a Meenies bomber jacket, a Laura Ashley party dress, a £50 computer game and a very expensive pair of red leather roller skates for Christmas. Was there any possibility, enquired my daughter, 'that you might deevolse Daddy for a bit'?

It is only when each side starts shacking up with others that the trouble starts.

A separated father who's bringing his children to lunch rings up and asks if he can bring his 'new lady' as well because she gets on 'so well with Natasha and Georgie'. Whereupon boot-faced children and teeth-gritting new lady roll up, both appalled at the prospect that she may be their new stepmother, with the father totally oblivious of any tension.

One of the main problems for children is divided loyalties. Will their mother, who hasn't remarried, be desperately lonely if they spend Christmas with their father who has? They don't like their new stepmother that much but she's frightfully rich so the pickings might be good.

Will they be pumped to death on their return? 'Oh, he gave you a colour telly did he? Must be doing well,' says their

mother, making a mental note to ask for more mainten-
ance.

Trouble often starts too, when a second husband arranges
to deliver presents to his children at his first wife's house. Nervous of his reception, he gets tanked up beforehand and, with
parcels slightly damp from the bar counter, arrives at the
house, has a few drinks, and, in the relief of not fighting with
his ex, loses all sense of time and doesn't get home until
midnight – to find his second wife in hysterics.

Rows flare up, too, at Christmas because the remarried wife
is so determined that her children shouldn't feel deprived that
she neglects her new husband. 'She won't put a lock on the
bedroom door – our sex life is a shambles,' grumbled one stepfather.

But these things can cut both ways. One stepchild told me
that the worst thing about Christmas was having to open her
stocking on the bed in which lay both her mother and stepfather.

Another agony for stepchildren is to see their parents getting
wrapped up in a new young family.

'I'm desperately jealous of my two stepbrothers,' admitted
one girl, 'Not only are they in a happy family, and my father
and stepmother absolutely dote on them, but they seem to get
far more presents than I do, and, worst of all, the baby's got
my old room.'

Other steps are upset because their father – probably pres-
sured by their stepmother – doesn't seem so keen to have
them for Christmas any more. 'We missed not his presents but
his presence,' wrote Nancy Sinatra sadly about Frank, her
father.

Even worse is the tragedy of the older stepchild who is so
bolshy and bloody-minded that neither side wants him for
Christmas.

'My newly married stepmother was cooking Christmas
dinner,' said one teenager. 'She told me to get out of the way
because it was her kitchen now. On Boxing Day, she threw
me out because I reminded her so much of my Mum. Next
year I went to my Mum's; she'd got a new baby, they were
all over her, I got jealous, and there was a row. You could
see the relief on my stepfather's face because he had a really

'We couldn't afford to drink
when he was married to me!'

good excuse to throw me out because I was upsetting my Mum.'

Pity, too, the fate of one unfortunate stepchild whose parents live close to one another, and who has to eat two Christmas dinners, one at lunchtime with his father and new wife, and another in the evening with his mother.

Stepchildren, of course, can play on the situation and be absolute monsters. One sees them muttering together in covens at Christmas drinks, with the stepmother pathetically trying to behave as though everything's normal. Another friend, whose stepdaughter was at a country boarding school, took a day off work to drive down to the child's carol service, because the mother, who didn't work, was too lazy to go. When she got there, the child refused to speak to her.

It's also exhausting for the stepmother at Christmas, when money spread over two families is very tight, and, in addition to looking after her own young children, she has to cope with three sullen steps as well.

'They're absolutely livid if all the presents aren't levelled up,' said one stepmother, 'and their mother sends a list of the clothes they've brought (which I'm sure they deliberately lose), and then expects them returned clean. I spend most Boxing Days washing and ironing.'

The tragedy is that children long to admire their parents, but often at Christmas see them behaving worse than ever. Last Christmas, I heard one friend referring to her husband's ex-wife as an 'old frump with a wing-commander moustache', in front of her stepchildren. And one first wife, when her ex came to pick up their daughter for Christmas, insisted that he put a towel over the passenger seat as 'I'm not having my child sit where That Woman has sat.'

Another first wife, whose husband has made a very happy second marriage, always insists on having a drink with him and his wife on Boxing Day.

She kicks off by telling him how much he's aged and put on weight, then when offered gin or whisky says: 'Oh a real drink, I wish I could afford spirits.'

Then she comments on all the *new* chair covers which are actually five years old and the new pictures, and finally when her ex stumps out in a rage, turns sympathetically to the second wife saying, 'I'm sorry he hasn't got any easier.'

Whereupon the second wife retaliates by saying: 'And I can see exactly why he left you.'

What is the answer? Even though it's often impossibly difficult, try and see the other person's point of view. Remember that a first wife may be jealous at seeing her children having fun with someone else, that a second wife may be jealous of the offspring from a previous marriage, that most teenagers are bolshy at some time, and that all older children are jealous of affection lavished on baby brothers and sisters. And don't blame it too much on yourself or the step situation.

Christmas – if we feel we've been beastly to our stepchildren in the past – does at least give us a chance to try again, and to remember that a partner's or a parent's love will grow rather than decrease if one is prepared to share it. Remember that St Joseph was a stepfather, and it must have been quite denting to his macho to follow God as a first husband. Perhaps he was canonised because he fulfilled an almost impossible role with dignity and affection.

The childless

Since Christmas is allegedly a special time for the children, it is a particularly agonising season for couples who are trying to or cannot produce offspring.

After six years of marriage, and countless corrective operations, I remember being in such despair one Christmas, because my mother-in-law kept going on about there being no more Coopers to carry on the line, that I drank too much sherry at Boxing Day drinks, and passed out over the turkey left-overs at lunchtime.

People assume, quite mistakenly, that it cheers up the childless to be surrounded by little nieces and nephews at Christmas, or to be asked over to watch a neighbour's children open their presents, or to be roped in to help with a children's Christmas party. It is, in fact, torture.

What they want to see is their own children's eyes lighting up at the sight of the Christmas tree, not anyone else's. That is why childless couples so often opt out of Christmas and go abroad.

Pets

There came wise dogs from the East bearing bones, and being wise they ate them.

Many English people won't go away at Christmas because they can't bear to abandon their animals. They hate the thought of putting the dogs in kennels, where they won't get any turkey left-overs or a paper hat to wear at Christmas dinner, or leaving the cat in a cold house, with a neighbour coming in every day to top up the untouched Whiskas.

Other people have to work hard looking after farm animals. I remember one farmer's wife telling me that she was going to have a lovely Christmas, because for the first time in thirty years of marriage they didn't have cows to milk.

At midnight on Christmas Eve, holly is supposed to blossom and the cattle go down on their knees, with tears running down their furry faces – not only perhaps to honour the birth

of Christ but because so many of their little calves are tied up
in factory farms unable to kneel, or even turn round.

Pets like their owners, tend to behave very badly at
Christmas: dogs cotton on to the leg-lifting potential of
Christmas trees in the high street, and slaver to get their teeth
into a new consignment of plastic stocking fillers and bedroom
slippers. One year, my young niece made neat parcels of Go
Cat for their three cats, and hung them on top of the tree.
The whole tree crashed down twice before my sister-in-law
discovered why the cats were rushing up to the top of it and
tearing at the parcels.

Underwalked and bored, Maidstone, our English setter, was
always running away during Christmas week. One Christmas
day when he had done this and we were tearfully opening our
presents, imagining him under a non-existent bus, we got a
telephone call from a house in Roehampton, several miles
away, saying that Maidstone had enjoyed a turkey dinner and
eaten everything except the sprouts, and was now watching
the Queen's speech.

These days at Christmas dinner, when they're not out on
the razzle, our dogs wear bows, and have presents; chew sticky
bones, or squeaky cutlets or buns, which they chew until the
squeak falls out – a squeak-ectomy my husband calls it. One
dog usually retreats upstairs in a sulk because of the crackers
popping. The cats have catnip mice.

A teenage friend reports that her dog Dino sensibly fasts on
Christmas Eve, even allowing the puppy to eat his dinner,
because he realises that it's Christmas, and there will be heaps
of good things for him on the morrow.

On Boxing Day, when our dogs are so podgy from overeating that they have to jump sideways through stiles, the cats
mount an assault on the turkey carcase. Putting an Ascot-hat
meat-safe cover over it is quite useless because a claw fits neatly
into one of the mesh holes, and can be hooked off. One year,
we went to the trouble of weighting down our meat safe, but,
frantic with greed, the senior cat gnawed her way through the
mesh.

As little children grabbing nuts and sweets always leave the
larder door open, my nephew last year had the bright idea of
rigging up a rope tied to the mud weight from a boat, so that

the door closed very slowly even when left wide open. The cats soon worked this out, and spent Boxing Day playing last one out is Chicken – or rather Turkey. The pantry is freezing and they don't like being shut in, so often they mistimed their exit and got their tails caught.

A terrible bloody-mindedness overcomes cats when they are deprived of turkey. This Christmas one of ours could be seen halfway up the bird-table stand, furiously shaking the bread off the platform above, while her kitten hovered in the bushes below in case an unwary robin darted down to pick up a crumb. Other occupations included crash-landing on furniture among the Christmas cards.

Kennel guests, brought to stay at Christmas, are seldom very popular: Granny's Peke, who yaps and has dirty un-clipped paws which spread mud all over the newly scrubbed kitchen floor; big dogs that lift their legs on the curtains, trail the wires of standard lamps like goose grass, sweep tea cups off small tables with wagging tails, and even worse chase sheep.

Nor does everyone coming to stay like the incumbent house animals. Barking dogs are very bad for Grandpapa's nerves and Granny always gets goosed by the Labrador. My husband's cousin remembers an ancient family cat who had a semi-permanent adherence on her backside of hair or worse, known as Pussy's bum-crumb.

'One Christmas morning,' she wrote, 'we appeared at breakfast to find Granny in a state of shock. She had left her hand-bag open on the kitchen table, and during the night, Pussy had somehow bitten off or removed her bum-crumb, which lay neatly across the middle of the bag.'

A friend remembers staying one Christmas with an aunt in Sussex who had a ghastly Jack Russell called Hengist who 'chewed up all our newly acquired gloves, rogered our new tights, and alternatively clawed or bit us. There wasn't much we could do in retaliation except give him the occasional surreptitious kick. One of my eighteen-year-old cousins who hated him most of all, however, vowed to get him and, finally, as we were leaving, he grabbed Hengist and shoved him in the fridge. Hengist survived to rot up further Christmases, but it was at least half an hour before his muffled frozen yaps were heard. Naturally, there were terrible accusations, and a great deal of bitterness, but we admired our cousin tremendously and never gave him away.'

A dog is for life, not just for Christmas

Never buy a puppy for the children at Christmas. It's the worst possible time to introduce a small creature into a new home with all the noise and excitement and tension. The children can easily get fed up with a puppy, too, when it starts eating their toys or making puddles, and little children, unless constantly watched, can be very cruel to animals if unused to them.

Tragically, Christmas is also a time when people go away, and, unable to be bothered to put their dogs in kennels, turn them out in the street, dump them in the country or, even worse, put them out on motorways. The majority of these poor animals end up in dog's homes and are put down; but sometimes there is a happy ending.

On Christmas Eve at the Evesham kennels of the National Canine Defence League two abandoned dogs were brought in: one, a beautiful young sheepdog bitch, the other a blind old mongrel, thin as a rake, with torn paws from desperate running. The kennel maids called them Mary and Joseph. After Christmas a home was soon found for beautiful Mary, but no one wanted poor blind Joseph; until some weeks later a newly married couple, actually called Mary and Joseph, came in looking for a puppy, but, moved by poor old Joseph's plight, took him home. A month later they asked if they could bring him back for a visit. The kennel maids were amazed to see Joseph jumping out of the car, and bouncing joyfully up to them. In a happy home he had regained his sight. All he needed was love.

The school holidays

How exciting! the children are breaking-up from school today. Scarlett has already collected little Nicholas and Carol from their primary schools, and is driving down to Berkshire to collect Holly from boarding school. Noël has taken the afternoon off to collect Robin from *his* boarding school. As usual, the end-of-term carol service takes twice as long as scheduled, and even the sight of pretty mothers in fur coats coming out of chapel doesn't cheer up Noël, who's been champing outside in the Volvo for forty minutes. Nor is his temper improved when he discovers that he needs a Pickfords van to ferry home all Robin's clobber, which includes a recently acquired second-hand hi-fi, a 6 ft by 3 ft piece of plywood and a moribund desk, which Robin bought off a boy for 50p. Noël drives home deliberately fast, so plywood and desk keep lurching forward concussing both Robin and Difficult Patch.

The euphoria of the first night home and roast chicken and Muscadet for dinner is marred only by Holly and Robin, deprived of tropical school central heating, shivering like whippets as they hug the Aga.

Next morning Scarlett and Noël really know that their children are home. Suddenly there's no hot water. The paper is missing because it's up in the television room. Telephone book, hair dryer and shampoo also vanish without trace; so do most of both parents' clothes. Dirty washing festers in trunks and is occasionally hauled to the surface like bits of the Mary Rose, because it needs to be washed and ironed before lunch. The cardboard opening to the orange juice is soggy from so many people drinking directly from the carton. There are teeth-marks in the cheese, and strips of ham fat like some vast truncated tapeworm lie in the fridge because all the lean has been torn off. Meals, on the other hand, are hardly touched, although half a ton of chocolate, and twenty-five satsumas a day are consumed between times. The word 'satsume' ought to be coined to mean 'consume maniacally'. Somehow, too, Holly and Robin always seem to be missing when Scarlett is about to ask them to stay in and babysit for Nicholas and little Carol, when she and Noël want to go out.

Noël is deeply impressed by journalists like Terence Brady, who write in the *Daily Mail* that children enjoy Christmas far more if they are involved in helping and cooking. Mr Brady suggests, for example, that they should be put in charge of a Christmas Day breakfast of bacon, poached eggs on a toasted

muffin topped with white sauce. Such culinary skill is way
beyond Robin and Holly, who, when they cooked lunch once,
put on the cabbage three hours early. Instead, at Christmas
there is Noël's pep talk, which begins, 'Your mother and I
have no wish to work ourselves into the ground this year.
Everyone will muck in.'

After an appalled silence, tasks are delegated. Holly will
hoover the drawing-room, sweep the kitchen floor, and unload
the washing-up machine every morning; Robin will light and
maintain the fire.

The system never works. By the time both teenagers have
surfaced at midday, usually deathly pale, with flopping, newly
washed hair, all tasks have been completed by an exasperated
Scarlett.

Money doled out for Christmas present shopping is immediately spent on clothes for the recipient. More is requested and
refused.

'Why can't I have an allowance like my friends?' storms
Holly.

'Because I didn't have an allowance until I was sixteen and
you're only fourteen,' says Robin crushingly.

And the row follows its normal deafening course.

Another shorter argument goes:

Holly: 'Can I have £20 to go to a ball in London?'
Scarlett: 'No.'
Holly: 'I know a boy who can forge tickets.'
Scarlett: 'Oh, all right then.'

One of the most wonderful things about teenage girls last
Christmas was that they dressed in black from top to toe from
morning till night, which meant absolutely no washing for
four weeks. Scarlett cannot understand the older generation
chuntering about black on the young. She always says to
Holly: 'You're too young *not* to wear black.'

Parents

Ding-dong unmerrily on Earth.

It must be said in Holly and Robin's defence that parents are
not themselves in the weeks before Christmas. Scarlett will be

resentful, completely exhausted, suffering from Pre-Xmas Tension, emotionally susceptible to the slightest hiccup, and liable to fly off the handle or burst into tears at any moment. Noël will be almost as bad. Exhausted, suffering from alcoholic poisoning after a spate of office parties, guilty about not working enough, horrified by the cost of Christmas, held up by appalling traffic jams, he staggers home to find the house looking like an Advent calendar, with all the lights blazing and every door open to admit howling gales.

Nor, after a blazing row with Scarlett, can he storm out of their bedroom over Christmas and sleep in the spare room, because his in-laws will soon be ensconced there. Their disapproving presence also means that he has to shave every day, and that he can't vent public rage on Scarlett or the children.

Noël, who's a slob, will spend most of the festive season snoring under a newspaper in front of the box, and getting very put out when papers to snore under aren't delivered on Christmas and Boxing Day. Between kips, rather like the newly deserted wife, he announces that he's shattered, ill and doesn't want to see Anyone At All over Christmas. Five minutes later a crony rings, and he's joyfully off to the Dog and Trumpet for a Christmas drink.

'Christmas drink' is a word like 'duck', 'lion' or 'pheasant' that implies the plural.

Health

In England, according to a doctor I spoke to, not only do people's marriages break up over Christmas, but many patients go mad. People who manage to stagger through the year without needing a doctor lose their balance completely. Parents also bring Kevin, Tracey, Shelley or Barry in to the surgery before Christmas as a precaution, 'Just in case he's ill next week, doctor.'

An English psychiatrist told me that she always has twice as many patients in the week before and the week after Christmas. In America hostility to Christmas is regarded as a recognisable pathological symptom. Alastair Cooke reported that many psychiatric patients become seriously depressed before Christmas and do not recover until the season is over.

'Asleep? More like looking at page three!'

'They react,' he wrote, 'With outbreaks of hives, overeating, crying jags, dishonesty, sexual deviation and plain orneriness. Their depression continues until they are relieved of the pressure to be happy.'

What is the best way of staying healthy over Christmas? The experts divide into two camps. The optimists, who include Dr Malcolm Carruthers, President of the Society of Psychosomatic Research, claim that making merry is a protection against heart disease and that having a good time is far better for us than worrying about the effects of the Christmas binge. According to Dr Carruthers, unwinding, enjoying yourself, and letting go of tension all help to cleanse the body of toxic fat.

In the other corner are the gloom merchants, who say that most of us suffer from festive fallout, i.e. bad temper and melancholia at Christmas, and quite mistakenly counter it by stuffing ourselves with food and drink as our only refuge from emotional conflict.

The truth lies probably somewhere between the two. We all perk up after a few drinks, and it's very easy to be the life and soul of the party if you fill yourself with booze, but after a few days of it you start feeling terrible.

Alastair Cooke reported one American psychiatric patient who yielded to his 'exhibitionist-voyeuristic impulses' by spending Christmas every year in a nudist colony. This seems a splendid, if chilly, idea. With all those people staring at you and no huge sweaters to hide the festive midriff fall-out you couldn't let yourself put on weight.

For me, and I suspect many women, the greatest contributory factor to Christmas gloom, after exhaustion, is feeling fat. With the temptations of nougat on the kitchen shelf, brandy butter in the fridge, Christmas cake in the larder, chocolates in the hall drawer, crystallised fruits in the television room, it's all too easy to put on three quarters of a stone in ten days. The answer is to buy one ravishingly glittery dress before Christmas, at least one size too big, because it's bound to fit by New Year's Eve, and low cut, because tits, if nothing else, tend to get better when you put on weight.

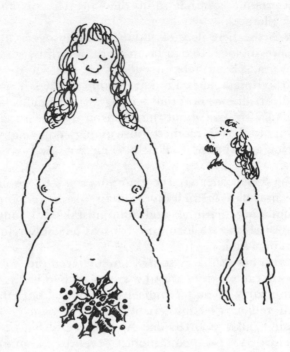

Nudist colony Christmas

Stockings

My heart leaps up when I behold a reindeer in the sky.

Now the children have broken up, it's time for a trip to Santa's Grotto. In Stroud this year, it only cost 50p for a visit and a present, and you could have your photo taken with Santa as well.

Playing Father Christmas these days is a pretty taxing job. In department stores, Santas must never ask a child how Mummy and Daddy are, because so many parents are divorced, and long explanations hold up the queue. Instead he must ask, 'How are the folks?' Nor must he say 'Yo Ho Ho'

as it frightens the children; or mention chimneys because most
kiddies haven't got one; nor wear spectacles; and if asked
where Rudolph is, he has to say 'miles away', or the kiddies
will mob the car park looking for him.

The Santa School near Swindon insists on clean fingernails
and no smoking or drinking because it makes the breath smell.
Santas must also be hale enough to lift 200 children a day,
and sharp enough to field requests like, 'Can I have a race
horse?' or 'Will you bring me a twin baby sister?'

Santa's life, in fact, is not a happy one. He often gets peed
on, children make a point of stamping on his feet as they
clamber on to his knee and, as one Father Christmas replied
when asked why he was wearing shin pads: 'If the little sods
didn't get something they asked for last year, they come back
this year and kick the hell out of me.'

Stephen Pile had the wonderful fantasy that all Santas were
members of the NUJ writing their Christmas pieces.

Occasionally Santa hits back. Last Christmas I saw one
turning the air as blue as the flame round the Christmas
pudding, because he couldn't get a taxi in Piccadilly. Others,
according to the *Sunday Telegraph*, have boxed the ears of re-
calcitrant children, fought among themselves over a street
corner pitch, and been hauled up because they spent more
time peering into the ladies changing-rooms than dispensing
Christmas cheer.

In Russia, where there is a five-rouble visiting Santa Service, he is called Father Frost. Usually he gets plastered on
vodka tots on the way, and seldom makes later appointments.
In Islington, most Santas are women who don't need false
beards.

Hardly surprisingly – not all children like the idea of the
Red at the end of their bed. One little girl asked her mother
to hang her stocking outside the door, as she didn't want
strange men in her room.

My niece, Clemency, was totally convinced from the age of
four that Father Christmas was a member of the IRA and was
absolutely terrified of him. According to my sister-in-law, 'She
not only wouldn't hang her stocking in her room, but also
barricaded both ends of the corridor. We used to dread
Christmas in case she caught sight of Father Christmas in a

shop, as she would dive under the counter, screaming at the top of her voice.'

On discovering that Father Christmas was in fact her mother, my niece got over this prejudice, and not only hung up a stocking herself, but left three dolls sitting in a neat row, each with an empty sock in their hands, thus blackmailing my sister-in-law into filling the lot.

The luckiest five children I know have a collossally fat feminist mother whose tights would be loose on an elephant. Her hen-pecked husband is less lucky. Not only is he allotted the task of filling these vast pairs of tights (last year it took him until four in the morning) but each one cost him £50 to fill.

Customs vary. Princess Diana uses old hunting socks of

Prince Charles, filling them with an apple, an orange, a bag of sweets and a small toy; which certainly wouldn't have satisfied actress Nerys Hughes' son, Ben, who hung out a pillowcase and six socks one year, and they were all filled. Next year, he left a 'duvy' because the presents he wanted were rather big.

Some parents prolong the illusion by really entering into the spirit of the thing, leaving mince pies and even whisky and nuts for Father Christmas and carrots for the reindeer.

'I'm sure I stopped my children going to sleep,' said a friend, 'by imagining that I heard sleigh bells, and dashing outside with the children to search the sky, and putting sooty footprints on the drawing-room carpet.'

Conversely, a woman friend claims that an infallible way of making small children behave and go to sleep early on Christmas Eve is by telling them that if they don't you'll telephone Father Christmas and tell him not to come.

Once your child twigs that Father Christmas doesn't exist there's no getting away with arguments like that, or the argument that he couldn't possibly get ponies and record-players down the chimney. Children usually learn who Santa really is from elder brothers and sisters or other children at school, or because delivering parents are not as sober as they might be. My sister-in-law rumbled the truth when her father fell down the two steps into her bedroom, and dropped the stocking: 'I woke to find him crawling round, swearing furiously, trying to stuff the parcels back in again.'

'My eternal problem,' said a girlfriend, 'is that over-excited children seldom sleep before 2.00 a.m., so I've spent many endless exhausting Christmases creeping in and out of a blackened room trying to see if the little bleeders' eyelids have finally dropped.'

Also, if one is foolish enough to put sweets or chocolates in the stockings, they'll all be devoured by reveille at 5.30 a.m. This means that the children aren't at all hungry at breakfast, but ashen-faced, cross and starving long before the turkey is ready.

I have to confess that my own nadir at Christmas used

always to be 2.00 a.m. on Christmas morning. I would battle
to the end of the Christmas Eve rat race, which invariably
involved buying all the stocking presents, getting tight at my
husband's office party, tearing back to Putney – usually to
find that some ancient relations had arrived early and been
parked outside the house for hours – getting them and the
children through dinner and to bed, going to midnight
mass, and returning usually still tight to tackle the tights.
Desperately wrapping presents in torn-up newspapers, I
could never remember which pair of tights was destined for
which child, so gave dolls to my son, and cap pistols to my
daughter (of which no doubt the feminists would have
approved) then, realising that I'd put two boxes of Rose's
chocolates into one stocking, would unpack the whole thing
and start again.

It's hardly surprising, after such cavalier treatment, that
my dear children never wanted to open their stockings very
early. But just as my husband was terribly sweet the year I
wrapped all the stocking presents in pages of his *Times Literary
Supplement*, which he hadn't yet read, my children never
seemed to mind that the tights they unpacked were never the
same colour as the ones they'd hung up, nor that Father
Christmas left all the prices on, or that he shopped at the
Tiny Set (our local toyshop) 'like you do, Mummy'.

It's hard to remember what presents were successful. But I
know that they liked body make-up, noisy musical instruments,
plastic fried eggs, expanding worms in tooth mugs, garden
gnomes in snow storms, paper fans, chocolate cigarettes, Lindt
chocolate kittens, glow stars and joke presents, so that they
could disappear and rush back giggling with huge orange ears,
protruding false teeth, and bloody bandaged fingers.

One of the greatest problems is balancing the stockings so
that each child gets a fair share. Even that doesn't always
work. My sister-in-law said that her two older children always
charged at everything, ripping the parcels open and finishing
in a few minutes, while the youngest child slowly and patiently
undid every parcel, viewed what was in it, played with it, and
then put it neatly in his box. The other two, convinced that
he'd got four times more than they had, sulked or punched
him as the mood took them. She can still remember her rage

as a child when my husband got a toy spitfire and she only a Wellington bomber – and the great relish with which she kicked him.

Stockings get easier as children get older. By the time our children were twelve and fifteen, we had to wake them up at ten o'clock on Christmas morning, because we couldn't bear to wait any longer to see how they'd react to their stockings. This year a serious imbalance in both quality and quantity of the stockings went quite unnoticed because my son unpacked his at midday, and my daughter hers at a quarter to one.

Christmas decorations

Man is born free but is everywhere in paper chains.

In a pathetic attempt to be more creative last year I got a book on Christmas decorations out of the library. I could have Christmas at my fingertips, the author advised me brightly, by learning how to make a simple evergreen corsage, how to decorate an *outdoor* tree, how to make my own candles, and, worst of all, how to give a gala air to breakfast on Christmas morning.

Having failed to achieve multiple snowflakes, I tried to make an aluminium reindeer. 'If your finished design is a direct physical likeness to a reindeer, it is unsuccessful,' said the author kindly, 'for it will not carry imagination on a significant journey.'

By the time I'd cut off two feet, a nose and an antler, and half an ear, there was no way that imagination or the reindeer was going to carry anyone anywhere and I gave up.

I turned to *Good Housekeeping*, who had some wild ideas about hanging baubles on your fatsia, sticking satin rosettes on your mother-in-law's tongue, and spraying aerosol on your rubber plants. As the last time that my son sprayed our sitting-room windows with aerosol snow we couldn't see out until August, I resisted this idea too.

If you have artistic skills and loads of time on your hands, it seems an excellent idea to employ them making elaborate Christmas decorations. Having neither, I prefer to tart up our house with huge clumps of holly and yew and trails of ivy, which all last better if you plunge them in water for a few hours after you've picked them. Mistletoe is essential too, hanging from a light in the hall, although it seldom has any berries left by the time you've fought your way back from the greengrocer's.

It is a status symbol in America to have two Christmas trees, one inside and one out. It is a status symbol in England to have a tree that touches the ceiling.

Christmas trees were first introduced by an English missionary called St Boniface. Riding through the forest in Germany, he surprised some pagans sacrificing a youth to a huge oak tree. Appalled, St Boniface grabbed an axe, felled the oak, saved the youth, then noticed a tiny spruce, growing among the roots of the oak. 'Let this small evergreen be your symbol of everlasting life,' he told the pagans, and from that day the spruce has been the centre of the German Christmas. Much later, in the nineteenth century, Prince Albert introduced it to England.

St Boniface would probably have taken another axe to some of today's artificial trees. For £5.99 in Woolworth's you can buy a gold tinsel model that collapses like an umbrella; or for £32.95 become the proud possessor of an 'instant, flame-resistant untarnishable, luxury, 6ft 8in 'pine' Christmas tree with tree-shaped lifelike branches, and realistic snow-covered needles.'

If you prefer the real thing, buy it in the market where trees are a third cheaper than in greengrocers or garden centres. Buy an English tree, as it will last longer, water it well – a few ice cubes in the earth every day work wonders – and keep it away from the radiator.

At Windsor, Prince William helps Nanny Barnes decorate the tree in the nursery of the Queen's Tower. Straw from the stables is placed round the charming tableau of battered biblical figures. A log fire burns all day, and the Guards band plays carols outside the window.

How harmonious when compared with the fearful squabbles that break out in our house. No one can ever find the box of decorations, so a great deal of time and acrimony is wasted looking for them. One fatal year, my son aged five, found the

'So Noël decided to save this year
by watering last year's!'

box first and triumphantly bore it off to school where he pre-
sented it to his beautiful form mistress. Having searched for
days, it was only when I rolled up for the end-of-term nativity
play that I at last found all our decorations adorning his
classroom.

The fall-out in Christmas decorations is also appalling.
Every year, since my children grew beyond the smash-and-
grab stage, my husband, who has some sort of death wish for
the decorations, has introduced a new kitten, who does the
job far more thoroughly. The minute you hang the first silver
bauble on the tree marks the opening of the volley-ball season,
and by evening everything is being batted all over the floor
and smashed to bits.

This year I toyed with the idea of buying 'shatterproof balls
made in Finland', but they were so ugly that I settled for the
gold angels and silver donkeys; my daughter said they were
'absolutely gross', which gave me a blissful excuse to sulk and
beat a retreat to the drawing-room fire with a large vodka,
leaving decorating the tree to everyone else.

As I hadn't bought a Woolworth's Christmas tree stand in
olive-green plastic 'with water contained to retard needle
drop', they had to make do with a bucket wrapped in foil.
This year's tree was too big for its bucket, and there was bitter
dissension between my husband and the children on the merits
of holding it down with earth or logs. Earth won, but only
after the tree had fallen over three times, smashed most of the
gold angels, and was finally secured by rope. As usual my son
waited until my daughter had decorated the tree to take
everything down and start again. Candles which we used
to have in the old days were so much prettier. Sadly now,
like fireworks, they are regarded as dangerous and generally
replaced by hideous fairy lights in primary colours in the shape
of lanterns, icicles or flowers. Remember whether your set
needs push-in or screw-in bulbs and get plenty of spares.

If you have young babies crawling around, do watch out
for scissors and wires; and, if you want to add glitter to
branches, use non-toxic paint. Ensure, too, that the open fire
has a really secure fireguard.

Last year, according to *The Observer*, white lights only were
de rigueur on the Christmas tree. In 1982, when we arrived in

Gloucestershire, I was firmly informed that it was fearfully common to decorate your tree with any colour other than blue. People were even white-washing their entire tree, and hanging only blue balls on it.

The tree in Trafalgar Square, sent by the Norwegians every year in gratitude for English support in the war, is lit a week before Christmas. Never arrange to meet anyone underneath it – you'll find 10,000 other people have had the same idea.

Never go and look at the lights in Regent Street either. My husband's aunt was shopping there when suddenly an eight-foot aluminium snowflake clanged to the ground and only just missed slicing her in half.

In Stroud last year we had bent choir boys, which was better than the year the plastic angels in Regent Street filled up with so much rain that they all looked pregnant. The only way to drain them was potting them with rifles – a shot-gun termination.

Three: The Dark Night Wakes, The Glory Breaks

Christmas Eve

Christmas Eve – and the excitement starts to bite. Little Nicholas and Carol, already in a frenzy of excitement, are opening the penultimate door of their Advent calendars. The wireless is playing a jazzed-up version of 'God Rest Ye Merry Gentlemen'. For Scarlett, there's not much rest ahead, but she hopes everyone will be merry.

Granny and Grandpapa arrived yesterday. Having been woken twice in the night, firstly by the departed neighbours' burglar alarm, and secondly by the lodger coming in tight at three o'clock in the morning, they are downstairs by 8.30 a.m., shivering, their breath rising like incense. Scarlett can't light a fire because the log man still hasn't arrived.

Leaving the children with their grandparents, she escapes after breakfast to do some last-minute shopping, and wishes she hadn't. Using holly as knuckledusters and Xmas trees as battering rams, shoppers are fighting their way ten deep along the pavement. Bad will is rampant.

At the supermarket there are no trolleys, because everyone's wheeled them five miles back to where they parked their cars and abandoned them. Scarlett wonders whether to start a home for Lost Trolleys.

'Mary was that mother mild', sings the loudspeaker, as inside the supermarket, mothers laden with loot bash and scream at older kiddies, and crash double prams of bawling twins into other prams. Terrible rows break out as last-minute presents are snatched from emptying shelves.

'I knew that carrier bag wouldn't 'old,' says a husband smugly, as a 100-ton oven-to-table lasagne dish, destined for

Auntie Hilda who's been learning Italian at evening classes, crashes to the ground on a toddler's foot, and the queue is held up for another ten minutes as some distraught cashier brandishes a red net of nuts which has lost its price tag.

'Shall I put on another Chippendale?'

In department stores, men are sweating at ladies' underwear counters muttering, 'I'm sure Sharon said a 25-inch hip'; and girls are fighting their way to the men's jerseys counter, wondering whether Trevor would look more macho in burgundy or pine green.

In every pub a rugger scrum of husbands, waiting to meet brothers-in-law, so that they can swap over carrier bags of presents for their respective families, is drowning its sorrows. At the prospect of going home to their visiting in-laws, their sorrows come up for the third time.

Outside it is raining. Other husbands, drenched and weighed down by carrier bags, like First World War pack horses on the way to the trenches, wait miserably for their wives who have disappeared and do not know where the car is parked.

*

At home, early on Christmas Eve morning, families committed to away fixtures gloomily listen to news of fearful traffic build-ups on every motorway. The children are fighting over who is to sit in the front. Ten miles down the motorway, the baby throws up all over Mummy.

Hours later at tea-time they reach Granny.

'Here you are at last,' she cries in fluting reproach, rushing out in her medium-heeled court shoes and wool dress, embracing gingerly as she inhales a waft of dried sick, trying not to wince, as older children tread mud all over the carpet.

Soon they're all into the obstacle race of family tea and Granny asking if anyone wants sugar, milk, a knife, jam, butter or a piece of Christmas cake. Her son-in-law, who's got sugar when he doesn't take it, is wondering how soon he can decently ask Grandpapa for a drink; the older children sit round in silence, already jittery because they can't monopolise the television and the telephone. There is a scream as the baby attacks the Christmas tree and the floor is soon covered with broken glass.

Over to mid-afternoon at the home fixture. Noël returns in a vile temper, hung over from several office parties, and aware that because of guilt and lack of time he has spent far too much on not very exciting Christmas presents. Seeing the tasteful holly wreath, trimmed with red ribbon and gold-painted kiwi fruits, hanging like a life-buoy on the front door, he wishes he could float away on it to oblivion leaving Christmas behind.

Depressed that he's not going to see Ms Stress for ten days, the sight of scurrying set-faced Scarlett doesn't make him any happier. He won't get any sex this side of New Year. Perhaps he too ought to buy a green plastic container from Woolworth's to prevent needle drop.

Now, as a final straw, he finds that Nicholas and little Carol are seriously in need of tranquillisers, and that Scarlett has barricaded herself into the kitchen stuffing the turkey, listening to the Festival of the Nine Lessons and Carols from King's College, which seems to come from a different planet of serenity and light. What can those angelic choristers know of the fever and fret of Christmas?

Noël's mother-in-law, after her night interrupted by drunken lodgers etc., is having a rest, and his father-in-law wants to know which is the best route back to Petersfield on the day after Boxing Day, and what has happened to the cake tin with Battle Abbey on the lid in which they brought the home-made flapjacks. If only there were a test match to keep him quiet.

The old bugger is now looking at his watch, and saying he'd better go and rouse Mother, as it's Nearly Time for Tea. Some hope, mutters Noël, thinking of Scarlett, still stuffing in the kitchen.

Noël is dying to get drunk again, particularly as Scarlett's sister, her fascist husband and their out-of-control children, who are coming to stay for four days, are due any minute – which means that Noël won't have any pillows on his bed tonight. If only the older generation could get plastered as well, they wouldn't mind meals always being late.

Hearing screaming, Noël goes upstairs, where his children are killing each other, because Nicholas has eaten the sugar mouse Carol's teacher gave her for Christmas. Scarlett, having stuffed the turkey, has sneakily bolted upstairs and locked herself into the bedroom to wrap up her remaining presents. She had to grab the opportunity before the Sellotape, which is as elusive as Sir Percy Blakeney, went missing again.

Unfortunately, the Sellotape itself has already been extracted by some child from that contraption with a serrated edge that breaks the tape off where you need it. As a result, it is Scarlett's teeth which nearly break as the bloody Sellotape ridges, divides and crinkles, and finally merges into the pack, as she cocoons and papooses her presents.

One needs two people to pack presents, reflects Scarlett, as one does to stuff the turkey – or anything really. She has to re-open several of the presents to see what she put in them. She forgot to get any tags, and maddeningly Biro doesn't show up on that ludicrously expensive dark shiny wrapping-paper. She's been gift-ripped off again. If only she'd bought cheap paper, then at least she'd have a white Santa's beard, or a snowman's belly to write on.

Now she's even run out of paper; but she is not going to risk tin foil after last year when that scatter cushion for Aunt Margery got rammed in the oven by mistake. So she's reduced to pulling out lining paper from her chest of drawers. At least it's better than the year she got plastered and wrapped up her own boots by mistake, and nearly had to go to midnight mass in bedroom slippers.

More screams outside; Granny, unable to find the landing light on an urgent trip to the loo, has fallen down the stairs.

Next moment, the door bell rings and Scarlett's sister and fascist husband and the three monsters arrive at the same time as the log man.

A note for guests and hostesses

The hostess scurrying around at Christmas seldom feels the cold, but her guests will, particularly if they're old, and most of all if they're newly widowed or separated. It is essential to heat up the drawing-room, and have electric blankets or at least hot-water bottles and an electric kettle in the spare rooms. If you're the sort of hostess who can deputise, and is not distracted by chatter, heat up the kitchen so that people will gravitate there for warmth and you can get them grating onions or peeling sprouts.

Do stock up on loo paper, firelighters, hoover bags, and light bulbs (all ghastly if you run out). No one ever gets the milk right. You'll either have sixteen horizontal bottles hogging the fridge or run out on Boxing Day.

A friend who did the latter in the depths of the country filled up an empty two-litre vodka bottle with milk from a friendly neighbouring farmer. Putting it on the kitchen table, she horrified all the ancient relations by topping up their coffee with it at breakfast.

Ideal guests arrive and leave when they say they are going to, and come laden with goodies: a cold chicken, a garlic sausage, a large quiche, a game pie, an apple flan and lots of drink. Alternatively, if they're staying for a few days, they should cook the odd meal or take you all out to dinner. If they're getting a free Christmas, they can jolly well afford it.

The travelling granny who's coming by train, who can't carry much luggage, can always fall back on gardening, record or book tokens as presents. If she wants, and can afford, to contribute towards the food, she can always get a side of smoked salmon, a Stilton, a small hamper, or a few bottles of wine delivered to the house.

The hostess should watch out for, and note down, the odd food present that arrives by messenger or is dropped in by a neighbour, which can so easily disappear into the maw of the larder or the fridge and is never acknowledged properly thanked for.

Do remember how ultra-sensitive people are at Christmas: never criticise the food or the children. Grandparents, in particular, if they're having their family to stay, should distribute framed photographs of their grandchildren all round the drawing-room, with the ones of the visiting grandchildren to the fore. Praise and appreciation are crucial factors in making everyone have a happier Christmas.

When do you open your presents?

Lovers open their presents together before Christmas; the neglected open theirs when they arrive in the New Year. The Germans open theirs around six o'clock on Christmas Eve. The Royal Family, being largely of German ancestry and because they spend most of Christmas Day going to church, also open theirs on Christmas Eve. An eighty-foot-long trestle table in the Red Drawing-room is used to pile up the presents which are handed out by Prince Philip.

Because my maternal grandmother became pixilated with Prince Albert and all things German, it also became our family tradition to open our presents after dark on Christmas Eve. The tree, always more beautiful at night, was lit for the first time, and after opening we then had the evening ahead to play with our presents, leaving my mother free to stuff the turkey and pack up our stockings. It was my first real experience of hypocrisy. Having been through the present drawer with all the sensitivity of an airport frisker while my mother was shopping, I knew exactly what I was getting and had my gasps of simulated delight and amazement to perfection. My cousins, who were glamorous but lacked self-control even more than I did, had always bullied their mother into letting them open their presents by two o'clock in the afternoon.

Christmas Eve seems a sensible opening time. Having had one bite of the cherry, children are less frantic to wake up in the middle of the night and open their stockings, and with Christmas dinner still to come the goodies are more spread out.

When you open presents on Christmas Day depends on when you have Christmas dinner. In the old days, if you had it at lunch-time for the sake of the children, you upset the servants, who didn't like getting up at five in the morning to put the turkey in. But if you waited until evening to dine, you had to put up with fractious, exhausted children.

If you open presents after breakfast, it seems too near opening one's stocking; no one gets up at the same time, so you have to hang about waiting; you miss the beauty of the lighted tree; and you have to rush off to church immediately afterwards, or be plagued to assemble some plastic toy as you desperately try to get Christmas dinner under way.

If you open presents at midday, the children won't want to eat much Christmas lunch, because they'll be longing to get back to their presents. If you open them after lunch, you won't be able to linger at the table because the children will be so desperate to get unwrapping.

My husband's family used to open the bulk of their presents on Christmas night, after dinner had been washed up and breakfast laid, by which time I'd practically expired with anticipation. My husband remembers his parents having the same argument every year at Christmas breakfast when the children were young, when, as a sop to such a long wait until the evening, they were allowed to open presents from people who were immediate family. The row was always the same: 'Dad said my mother's mother wasn't family, and Mum said the aunts, my father's sisters, weren't, and a shouting match then ensued, year in year out.'

When I was first married my husband, thinking that opening presents on Christmas Eve was too decadent for words, made me stick to after dinner on Christmas night, but gradually over the years I and the children have worn him down to about four o'clock on Christmas Day, and then we dine at eight, which seems the best arrangement. Most people like what they've been brought up with and feel faintly martyred if a lifetime's routine is changed.

'What do you mean, you can't remember who sent it?'

Only open your presents in the privacy of your own family. Everyone reacts to Christmas in different ways. Some people go berserk and give each other hundreds of presents, from the dogs, the cats, the fox in the woods and the goldfish, but some don't. There is nothing more embarrassing than opening a pile of presents in front of someone else who has nothing. Princess Diana very sensibly avoids the mass opening in the

Red Drawing-room and opens presents alone with her children.

Do remember to leave the bills in 'by mistake', then everyone can change everything next week.

If you all have lots of presents from different people, make a chart before you start and as each present is opened, write down who it came from, as by Boxing Day you won't remember, which makes thank-you letters very embarrassing.

Some people remove half the presents from very small children and dish them out during the year in times of crisis. This sounds a good idea, but it never works with my children who have memories like computers, when it suits them, and would have instantly missed the smallest toy.

Don't be too hasty to throw away the wrapping-paper. I've lost several silk scarves and gift tokens that way.

Always keep a few spare presents back in case you need one for the ghastly dropper-in who arrives on Boxing Day, laden with goodies. I bet Mary cursed the wise men when they caught her on the hop in January.

Church

> *And is it true? And is it true,*
> *This most tremendous tale of all,*
> *Seen in a stained-glass window's hue,*
> *A baby in an ox's stall?*
> *The Maker of the stars and sea*
> *Become a Child of earth for me?*

John Betjeman

One of the eternal debates for the noble army of churchgoers on Christmas Eve is whether to go to midnight mass, early service or matins on Christmas morning. However tired I am, I prefer the former, for the shaming reason that it gets church over with, and because, even more shamingly, if I opt for early service or matins the next day I never make it, and spend the rest of Christmas feeling guilty and somehow as though spiritually I'd gone to bed without cleaning my teeth and taking my make-up off.

'I suppose you're too tired for midnight mass
and too emotional for matins tomorrow!'

The French very sensibly have the incentive that after midnight mass they sit down to a massive blow-out called *le reveillon*, in which they consume baked ham, roast chicken, salads, cake, fruit, bon-bons and lots of wine. In Alsace they have goose; in Paris oysters and a cake shaped like a yule log, as well as champagne and dancing. These revelries carry on all night, rather like our New Year's Eve. This balanced, materialistic race also emphasise the secular nature of Christmas by including the policeman, the mayor, the priest, the butcher and the baker among the figures in the crib.

The Poles, on the other hand, have a twelve-course dinner on Christmas Eve. No meat is allowed, so eight kinds of fish are consumed, including caviar, salmon and carp, followed by borsch, pudding and cakes, with each course washed down with vodka and wine. After such a splendid banquet, they drink Cognac and open their presents. After this, according to my beautiful Polish friend, who now lives in England, the trouble starts.

'At midnight,' she said, 'we all troop to mass, extremely the worse for wear. Throughout the vicar's sermon, my mother and aunt, since they don't understand what is being said, talk loudly in Polish on deeply religious topics such as:

' "I like your boots, Helena – where did you get them?"

' "Russell and Bromley in the sale."

' "How clever of you. Burgundy is such a difficult colour, isn't it?" '

Some people bribe their children into going to midnight mass by allowing them to open one present when they get home. Others have arguments about which church to go to: 'You can either come to the Catholic church with me, or go to the cathedral, which is being televised by the BBC.'

I always have to referee arguments between my children and my husband about hair not being brushed, and shirt tails hanging out. Rather invidiously, when you read about the Reverend Kilvert breaking the ice on his cold bath before setting out for church, my family always fight unashamedly for the seat by the radiator.

Any vain hope that I may get seduced by the beauty of the service is usually sabotaged by the clergyman taking it. The first year we moved to the country, the visiting vicar proceeded grumpily down the church to the early verses of 'Once In Royal David's City', and stopped in front of our pew to bless the crib. The organist, who appeared to be playing in boxing gloves, having paused for the blessing, started up again, whereupon the vicar snapped very loudly, 'Tell that idiot to belt up, I haven't blessed *him* yet,' so a vestmented choirboy had to beetle off to the organist, who ground equally crossly to a halt.

Later when we took communion the vicar kept muttering: 'Move up, move up on the rail, or I'll never get finished.'

But in a way that's better than the vicar who takes things desperately slowly, spinning his pep talk on peace and love out for half an hour, and packing in five carols, so that the congregation start sobering up and getting frantic for another drink. Invariably some drunk pulls a cracker or falls over and fuses the fairy lights, and teenagers get terrible giggles because one of their interminable yawns turns into a belch.

The good thing about midnight mass is that apart from giving you a chance to thank God for helping you survive another year, it does provide you with an opportunity to discover if any new talent is staying in the area over Christmas. Who would have thought, marvels Scarlett, that Mrs Piggott from the Old Rectory would have such ravishingly handsome teenage grandchildren? Perhaps she might now even be able to persuade Holly and Robin to accompany her and Noël to the Piggotts' for drinks on Boxing Day.

Because of the possible invasion of new talent, and because everyone has so much time to stare at everyone else, it's as well to look presentable at midnight mass. One local wife very chicly matched a purple coat to a purple black eye last year.

Clean hair is also a good idea, because the overhead lights really show up the scurf and grease. And do wipe the mud off the heels of your boots, which'll show when you kneel down at the altar. Don't forget your collection.

One of the reasons people shun church on Christmas morning is because they can't get decent matins any more. Instead, you are subjected to the inevitable sung eucharist, often larded with pop songs in the more progressive churches and all the congregation joining hands in ghastly chains of communication. My husband always stands with his arms grimly folded like an All Blacks rugger player, so that no one on either side can shake hands with him.

If you can persuade your husband to take the younger children to matins, it will at least give you an hour and a half of peace to prod the turkey and nurse your hangover. But sadly, there is nobody more sanctimonious and nit-picking than members of your family returning from a church service which you have not attended. At least if you don't go to midnight mass you can pretend to be asleep when they get home.

Christmas dinner

In for a pinny, in for a pounding.

The kiddies, sleeping peacefully beside their unopened stockings, are woken up by Scarlett O'Aga staggering downstairs, holding her hangover on with one hand, at five o'clock in the morning to put the turkey in the oven. As it's the size of an ostrich, getting it out of the Aga to baste it is like parking a pink car in a garage with millimetres to spare.

If you're having a frozen turkey, do let it unfreeze for three days. Do remember to take out the giblets. Don't spray the inside of the Aga with oven cleaner, and forget to wipe it off – as a friend did last year, so ten starving guests were greeted with a turkey indelibly impregnated with chemicals at midnight.

Don't make the ghastly mistake committed by another friend of thinking that the turkey would cook gently in the Aga overnight, and having to give the entire family Christmas breakfast. Beware the over-zealous husband, who manages to turn off the oven cooking the turkey, just before he and the family set out for a long round of Christmas drinks, so that they return to find the turkey still three hours off being ready. Do leave a hole in the foil so all the family can peer in and say: 'It doesn't seem to be doing at all.'

There are endless arguments over the merits of turkey *v.* goose. Goose is more chic and the fat makes brilliant roast potatoes, but it is also more sickly for small children, and feeds less people. The best cook I know stuffs her goose with truffles and leaves it in the summerhouse overnight. I hope that no one tips off the neighbouring foxes.

Now we're into the rat race of decorating the table. Granny in her own house spends hours finding matching crystal bowls for the chocolates, and she then can't remember where she's hidden them from the children.

My book on advanced decorating recommends that if you have a 'sophisticated group round the table, why not settle for a mirth-provoking centrepiece of Mr and Mrs Santa in a fresh situation.'

The author then goes really over the top and suggests you grace the centre of the table with 'an ice palace, built out of tin cans masked by silver foil, with snow drifting down, produced by a silver fan blowing against a packet of opened soap powder on the top shelf.' Persil washes white meat presumably.

On a simpler note, a red tablecloth with red candles, white

napkins and crackers, can look very pretty; so does a white tablecloth and candles with red napkins and crackers, or a similar combination of silver and gold. The size of your Christmas table decoration depends on how many people you have round the table.

It is important, we know, at Christmas to remember the stranger, the forgotten and the friendless. But if you ask outsiders in to Christmas dinner, do invite more than one. If the newcomer has to pick up the mood of a solid phalanx of family united by private jokes and animosities, he or she may feel lonelier than ever.

A friend whose father was a clergyman remembers that he always invited some unfortunate Singhalese boy to lunch who was miserably shy and had no presents to open.

'On another occasion,' she said, 'We had Miss Simon to stay, who came home from the mission field to attend Moorfields Eye hospital for treatment. During Christmas dinner her eye fell out on a tendon, and swung over her plate of turkey. Meanwhile we children were all under the table.'

Adrian Mole's Christmas dinner included his separated mother, his baby sister, a handicapped pensioner, two lesbians and the dog, which seems about par for the course.

But perhaps the worst guest at Christmas dinner is the one that really doesn't pull her weight.

'My sister stayed for three weeks,' said another friend, 'arriving seven days before Christmas. She did nothing, not even her bed, until the rest of the family arrived for Christmas dinner. Whereupon she immediately stationed herself at the oven looking haggard and sweaty. The family immediately went into raptures: ' "Oh how lovely – two sisters working together so hard to produce this fantastic dinner." I didn't speak to my sister for five days.'

Midday and Scarlett O'Aga, who is not very efficient, is beginning to feel overworked and flustered. Yesterday she made the brandy butter, the gravy and the potato croquettes, which only need heating up, and are so much less of a hassle than roast or mashed. But she still hasn't made the bread sauce, or done the sprouts.

'Oh Scarlett, do go upstairs, have a bath and relax!'

But it's advisable not to be too prepared. Added to the feeling of martyrdom that behind every turkey there's a knackered housewife, Scarlett does have the perfect excuse not to go into the drawing-room, where the rest of the family, having exhausted all the conversations about Gordon's marriage, or the possibility of Gwen's pregnancy, are beginning to get seriously on each other's nerves. Now that the invited lame ducks have arrived, conversation gets even stickier.

Little Carol and Nicholas, already bored with their Transformer toys, are clamouring to assemble that toy from Hamleys, which requires both batteries and glue, neither of which can be bought until the shops open. Noël wishes that he could transform his mother-in-law into Ms Stress. She has finished her one glass of sherry – the turkey won't be ready for at least two hours – and his father-in-law is asking directions to Petersfield yet again. Noël has read that at Christmas dinner at Queen's College they bring in a boar's head with an orange in its mouth. He wishes he could ram an orange into his fascist brother-in-law's mouth, to stop him pontificating on about the evils of being taxed at source.

In the kitchen, Scarlett is being taxed at bread sauce. Ignoring the recipe, she has added extra breadcrumbs because it seemed too thin, and now the whole thing's setting like cement. The turkey seems to be going backwards.

Noël shoves off to the pub on the excuse of getting brandy for the Christmas pudding, but really to ring Ms Stress. Getting her husband, Gordon, he loses his nerve and is reduced to asking him, Ms Stress and their entire family to their Christmas party next week, which he will somehow have to square with Scarlett. It's hardly the right moment now she is carrying a swimming pool of spitting turkey fat from the oven to the sink, and spitting even more because her sister, having done nothing to help, has just emerged, ravishing in a new pale blue cashmere Christmas cardigan. Scarlett hasn't even had time to change, and the Crème puff kept in the kitchen cupboard, on *Woman's Own*'s advice, to tone down a flushed face is proving utterly useless.

As a final straw, the cat has got into the dining-room and eaten the smoked salmon off two plates. Spreading it around again, hoping that no one will notice, Scarlett longs to leave

home. Then they'd be sorry. But alas, mini cabs are double
fare over Christmas, and she'd never get one anyway.

In the drawing-room, Granny has a completely wet sleeve
from putting her hand over her glass to stop her fascist son-
in-law filling it up with Noël's champagne. At least there are
sounds off of Noël carving.

In hospitals, surgeons, presumably the best carvers in the
world, put on fancy dress to do the honours. Never offer to
carve in someone else's house. One stockbroker, not famed
for his tact, was spending Christmas with his mother-in-law
and her new husband, Algy, who was in his seventies.

'Just as we were going in to dinner,' said the stockbroker,
'Algy made some crack about a friend of mine. I shut him up
and said I wasn't going to have my friends insulted. Seeing
Algy looking a bit bleak, and because being brought up in
the war he carves jolly thin slices, I offered to carve for him
and took over.

'Twenty minutes after we'd sat down to dinner we realised
that Algy wasn't there. He'd gone to bed in a sulk and refused
to come down again.'

Soon Noël has served everyone and, despite the fact that
most of the children and at least three of the adults are
drunk, and that short-sighted Grandpapa has mistaken a
holly leaf for a sprout, and is desperately trying to spit it out,
Scarlett feels almost happy when everyone drinks the cook's
health.

Everyone also oohs and aahs at the blue flame round the
Christmas pudding, except little Carol who, thinking the house
is on fire, dives under the table.

When I was young, children were lured into eating Christmas
pudding because of the possibility that inside they might find
silver sixpences, or the bachelor's button or the thimble –
horrors – which symbolised spinsterhood. Today's puddings
are often studded with £1 gold coins.

How long should Christmas dinner last? Several years ago
one frenetic temporary nanny hustled us through ours by
whisking away plates and refusing us second helpings in
thirty-five minutes flat. Conversely, a friend in Gloucestershire reports sitting down at 2.30 a.m. and not rising until

'Can we have it in front of the box?'

10.30 p.m., when everyone fell off their chairs.

Tangerines, chocolates, nuts, and expensive crackers with slightly more elaborate and expensive presents inside, can sometimes persuade both young and old to stay at the table longer. Granny's false teeth get lodged in a crystallised fruit. Everyone reads out riddles.

'What's the difference between a pillar box and an elephant?' asks Noël's fascist brother-in-law.

'Don't know,' says Noël.

'I wouldn't ask you to post a letter for me. Ha ha ha ha,' says his fascist brother-in-law.

Sparklers can also prolong the festivities, although hostilities will break out at the away fixture if some child leaves a white-hot remnant on Granny's sideboard.

At last, because the older generation want to watch the Queen's speech, washing up can be postponed no longer. This is the moment Granny in her own house has been longing for: hands, in rubber gloves, whisking round in the hot suds; 'glasses first please'; oh the relief of getting all the best plates, silver and glass put away; and the table laid for Christmas tea.

Now it's time for the Queen's speech. A male journalist friend got a very frosty negative recently when he asked Princess Margaret if the Royal family sat round watching her sister on television and afterwards each held up placards saying nine, seven, eight, two etc. to rate this year's performance out of ten. Last year, Mrs Thatcher, graciously addressing her peoples all over the Commonwealth, and the Queen, telling industry to get its finger out, seemed to have reversed their roles. Adrian Mole assumed that the Queen looked miserable because she'd had lousy presents like him.

Another male friend has vivid memories of being surrounded by his family, including his 88-year-old mother and several children, and settling down reverently to watch Her Majesty. 'Suddenly we all froze in embarrassment as the ram in the next-door field about fifteen yards away decided vigorously to perpetuate his species.'

After the Queen's speech, Noël suggests sending all the children out for a run round the village and offering £500 to the one who comes home last. Katharine Whitehorn more tolerantly recommends sending every member of the family, small, large, cheerful, drunk or sober, alone or together, to bed for the afternoon.

Alas, such siestas are generally punctuated by relations ringing up to thank you for your presents, and, sottish and stupefied, you have to rack your brains to remember what they gave anyone: 'Lucinda adored her rattle/T-shirt/book token/bottle of gin – this line's awful, what's the weather like your end?'

Another overwhelming piece of evidence that Christmas is not what it used to be is that there are no more pips except in grapes, and one can't end telephone conversations by saying in a high voice: 'There go the pips, darling.'

The best telephone story comes from Lady Cottrell, the wife of the master of Jesus College, Cambridge who wrote to *The Times* saying that some years ago she answered the telephone on Christmas day.

'Is that Jesus?' asked a voice.

'Yes,' replied Lady Cottrell.

Whereupon the caller sang her the entire verse of 'Happy Birthday To You', and rang off.

Games

One of the best ways to stop things going flat after Christmas dinner is to play games. If you have teenage children from different families staying, who don't know each other well, break the ice after supper on Christmas Eve by playing Consequences, which invariably gets lewder and lewder, followed by Charades.

I prefer the old-fashioned Charades in which everyone divides into two teams and raids Granny's dressing-up box in the attic – later poor Granny has to put everything back. Each team then privately selects a double-syllable word – 'wrapping', perhaps – and acts out three short sketches. During the first sketch someone has to, at some time, say the first syllable as in the sentence: '*Wrap* up warmly'. In the second sketch, they work in the word *ping*, perhaps: 'Her bra went *ping*.' In the final sketch one of the actors works the whole word, 'wrapping', into a speech. The other side then has to guess the word. There are always arguments and dictionary consultations because some smart alec claims that 'ping' isn't a real word.

Another even better ice-breaker is Russian Charades. Again you have two sides. One goes out. The other side stays in the room and thinks up a subject – 'Miss World' perhaps – which is told to the first person from the other side who comes in. He or she then has to bring in the second person from the other side and silently act out 'Miss World' to them. The second person then gets the third person in and silently acts out what he or she saw, usually with fearful hamming up and exaggeration – and so on, until the last person outside is brought in and has to guess the original subject; invariably they guess something completely different like Esther Rantzen giving birth.

More popular today but less fun is modern Charades, or The Game, as played in the television programme, *Give Us a Clue*, in which people have to guess the title of a book, a film or a play and where everyone gets frightfully competitive. One host was so anxious to win one year that he didn't even notice that his exhausted wife had fallen asleep on the floor in front of the fire, and a fallen log was singeing her hair. There are always a healthy number of young smartypants all too keen to catch you out with *The Persecution and Assassination of Jean Paul Marat as performed by the Inmates of the Charenton Asylum Under the Direction of the Marquis de Sade*.

A friend remembers staying in a large country house where one of the guests was a strange young man who had repeatedly tried to burn down his parents' stately home. The host, a great leg-puller, kept trying to feed in subjects like *Towering Inferno*, *Fire Down Below* and *The Matchmaker*. His brother-in-law, on the other hand, a celebrated homosexual, was given the eleven-word song, 'She wore an itsy-witsy, teeny-weeny, yellow poker-dot bikini,' and flounced out in a huff.

I remember an ex-starlet trying to interpret *California Suite*. After several dramatic entrances into the drawing-room (where we were all sitting, mystified) to indicate the word 'suite' with grandiose gestures, she swept out again, muttering, 'You lot wouldn't recognise good acting if it sat on your face,' never to return.

On the other hand, my eighty-year-old mother's enactment of a caterpillar on the floor is affectionately remembered by all her grandchildren as a 'new side' to Granny.

Another very good game which can be scaled down to any age group is Twenty-one Aces. The party sits round a big table with a set of poker dice. The person who throws the seventh ace, suggests a drink, Bovril and Bourbon perhaps, or Horlicks and Heineken. The person who throws the fourteenth ace mixes it, usually in sherry glass quantities, and the unfortunate person who throws the twenty-first ace drinks it, to howls of mirth.

A great success at office parties, and with all ages at home, is Squeak Piggy Squeak. Players sit in a circle. One player is blindfolded and given a cushion, and sits down on someone's knee. Without touching the victim, he then says, 'Squeak piggy squeak', and has to guess from the ensuing squeals and giggles who the person is.

A more sophisticated version, which we played very successfully at one of our Christmas parties but which only works if everyone knows each other, is Grope. Again, one of the party is blindfolded and sits down on a chair. One of the rest of the party is silently selected, and the blindfolded groper has to guess who it is by feeling them. Amazingly, wives and husbands seldom recognise each other – one can only assume that they make love with their eyes open and the lights on.

Board games like Mid-life Crisis, which tells you how to avoid divorce, can be tricky when marriages are under a strain at Christmas. Never play the Truth Game. Two married couples who were devoted to each other started playing it while out to dinner on Boxing Night. Husband Number One proceeded to tell Husband Number Two that he should lose weight; whereupon Husband Number Two told Wife Number One that she was a boring suburban housewife and ought to get a job; whereupon Wife Number One turned to Wife Number Two and told her that she had the most disturbed children in Putney; whereupon Wife Number Two turned to Husband Number One and told him that Wife Number One was being knocked off by Husband Number Two. The result was two divorces and neither couple ever speaking to each other again.

Unless everyone's very bright or good at general knowledge,
it's not a good idea to do the *Observer* or *Sunday Times* quiz as
a communal exercise. Someone's bound to be left with a feeling
of inferiority; and Grandpapa may well think again when he
realises that he's forking out £6000 a year of unearned income
to educate a grandchild who can't answer a single question.

'You shouldn't have asked Mummy to act "Turkey in the
Straw!" '

Trivial Pursuits, wildely popular at the moment, can also
lead to inferiority complexes. One Gloucestershire wife
solemnly sat down and learnt all the answers before
Christmas.

The latest refinement, Sexual Trivial Pursuits, which asks

players questions like 'What is a sequential orgasm?' or 'What is tribadism?' is a very bad family game, and ought only to be played with your own generation. A friend described her 78-year-old admiral stepfather thundering out his answers wearing a plastic rain hat acquired from a Harrods cracker and being listened to in amazement by two seven-year-old granddaughters. Don't get involved in a game if you want to get away from lunch before 7.30 p.m., or you'll be thought the most fearful spoilsport.

Noël's very favourite game at Christmas only needs two people. He and Ms Stress each sit down with a bottle of whisky and a glass. Both finish drinking their own bottle; then one of them goes out of the room and knocks on the door, and the other has to guess who it is.

Christmas televisions

Pre-video-us Albion.

Second only to the mega-catastrophe of the television breaking down (far worse than the collapse of the washing-up machine), the thing that makes people most ratty over Christmas is not being able to watch the programmes they want.

Were there fearful rows in the good old pre-telly days, one wonders, because the children wanted Daddy to read aloud from *The Christmas Carol*, and Granny insisted that Grandpapa recite 'The Night Before Christmas' instead?

During the Christmas holidays in any normal household Holly/Robin/Carol/Nicolas-won't-let-me-watch-my-programme arguments continue all day to the counterpoint of left-on wirelesses, tape recorders and gramophones blaring *fortissimo* throughout the house.

Matters become infinitely more acrimonious when Grandpapa, Granny, and Rich Great Aunt Phyllis, who are far worse telly junkies than the children, arrive, and insist on watching what *they* want – '*Bleak House* is so much better for you than *Dynasty*, darling.' – and the children, too awed, for once, to kick up, retreat to the kitchen and kick their parents.

Husbands get equally frustrated.

'My   mother-in-law,'   complained   a   neighbour   last

Christmas, 'goes on and on and on about what common voices all the newsreaders have, and the plethora of blacks and Jews on television, then, having insisted on watching *Tenko Reunion* rather than *La Traviata*, talks the whole way through the bloody thing.'

Before Christmas, in an attempt to defuse the warfare, Noël and Scarlett hire a video machine, which increases the rows one hundredfold, because one child gets a video film out of the library and insists on watching it twenty-four hours a day, so that the other children can't record the Christmas films they want to watch. From time to time there are screams of outrage, because 'Bloody Daddy's rubbed Madonna.'

Major rows also break out because Noël suddenly finds bits of the *Wizard of Oz*, or Sue Ellen having a shower in the middle of his new Christmas tape of *Don Giovanni*; or when, livid because Christmas dinner coincides with *Kiwi Fruit Kawana's Christmas Show*, Noël tapes it and, having settled down rather drunkenly to watch it at midnight, discovers that some child had switched the channels and recorded *Only Fools and Horses* instead.

A granny, however, who has young well-behaved grand-children coming to stay, and is racking her brains as to how to entertain them, could do a lot worse than hiring a video machine for a week, plus a dozen tapes. It costs very little. One friend who did it said that she hardly knew the children were there.

Three Christmases ago, there was a historic moment of harmony in our house for half an hour because both our children agreed that they wanted to watch a James Bond video on Christmas Eve. Proudly I brought back *For Your Eyes Only* from the video library. Alas, after five minutes of naked lesbian scuffling, I realised that I had acquired not James Bond but a blue film of the same title, which was hastily removed, to the children's fury.

It is as well to hide any blue films when Granny comes to stay – although a good meaty orgy might be an even better way of giving Rich Great Aunt Phyllis a coronary than *The Jane Fonda Workout Book*.

Anyone deprived of their favourite programme last year could at least bury themselves in the 160-page Christmas edition of the *Radio Times*, and read how caring comedians and chat-show hosts (photographed in August sweating in Santa gear, clutching gift-wrapped parcels with nothing inside them) would, even if they're in panto in the Shetlands, manage to snatch a few hours on Christmas Day, with their favourite woman: their Mum.

What people need during the festive season is the un-changing traditions. Christmas wouldn't be Christmas if we couldn't fall asleep in front of *The Magnificent Seven, Death on the Nile, The Slipper and the Rose* and *Ben Hur* yet again.

The only solution, so that everyone could watch and tape *everything* they wanted, would be to have four television sets and four video machines in everyone's bedrooms so that no one need meet over Christmas at all. Perhaps the whole family should do an exchange with some television wholesaler, who wanted a quiet Christmas.

Four: But What Comes After . . .

'Would it do for next Christmas, darling?'

Boxing Day

According to a doctor, the best day to be on call over the festive season is Christmas Day. Hardly anyone is ill: they all manage to postpone their heart attacks, bouts of flu, and appendicitis until Boxing Day, when the surgery is like the first day of the sales.

Boxing Day is also the time when anarchy breaks out in families, because there are no formal Christmas activities to distract people. My beautiful Polish crony, for example, reports that in 1984 the husband and father of a friend of hers mysteriously went missing for the whole of Boxing Day, and were finally run to ground locked in a heated greenhouse with a bottle of whisky and a week's newspapers.

'My new mother-in-law,' admitted a male friend, 'just managed to behave herself until Boxing Day, when she spent the whole time picking on the children from my first marriage, and pointing out how pathetically slow they were at Scrabble compared with my stepchildren, at whom she smiled with deep, understanding sympathy every time I raised my voice.'

The upper classes, of course, work off their Boxing Day aggression by murdering wildlife: many of them go shooting. Others attend the Boxing Day meet, with everyone capping everyone else's hangover stories, and grannies, after an indigestion-interrupted night, telling their friends with rather less conviction what fun it is to have a houseful. Often the Master's leftie daughter joins the Antis and knots everything up.

It's a pity that the middle classes can't exhaust their Box

Day spleen in organised boxing matches, with Grandpapa in
the dark blue corner, still asking the best route to Petersfield,
doing ten rounds against Rich Great Aunt Phyllis, the south
paw in the red corner.

Post coitum, omnia animalia triste sunt. After the orgasm of
cooking Christmas dinner, poor Scarlett, wearily sweeping up
a rubble of cracker mottoes, streamers and spat-out over-
rummed truffles, is filled with despair at the prospect of turkey
left-overs. Perhaps her fascist brother-in-law will demand
right-overs.

Noel's Fascist Brother-in-law

Noël, thinking of leg-overs, and deciding to ring Ms Stress,
slopes off to the Dog and Trumpet, which is crammed with
people, so euphoric at having got rid of their in-laws or their
grandchildren that they are buying gallons of whisky for everyone. He returns plastered at 2.30 p.m. and, passing the village
shop, misreads the date for Christmas week dustbin collection,
and insists that Scarlett puts out all the dustbins that night.

Boxing Day is appropriately named because hopelessly

overtired, whining children keep asking their parents what they can do, and on being told sternly that they've got a Whole New Nurseryful of Toys, answer, 'So what?', and get their ears boxed.

In the afternoon, good fathers lock themselves into the nursery to play with the train sets they've given their children, or try to assemble toys, which turn out absolutely nothing like the picture on the box. Others try to assemble kites, but alas there is no wind, except in them; or, if there is, the kites get lodged high up in the trees, and the fathers break their ankles trying to get them down, and join the last day of the sales at the doctor's surgery.

Noël, by now trying to sleep off his hangover in front of the telly, is constantly interrupted by the shrill piercing voices of his children, and wonders why on earth Herod held off until 28 December to slaughter the innocents. Outside the sky is suddenly heavy with impending snow, but not as heavy as Noël's heart at the terrifying possibility that his in-laws may be snowed in, and not able to take any route home to Petersfield tomorrow.

Just as he's dropped off, the door bell goes. It's droppers-in – the enemy of droppers-off; usually a separated father who's got his children for Boxing Day and would rather they broke up Noël's place than his.

On Boxing Day, according to the *Sunday Telegraph*, Victoria Gillick and her husband bundle their ten children into a van and drive round the country dropping in on friends – like a sort of do-it-yourself Arnhem. Imagine the horror of having racing at Kempton interrupted by an implosion of Gillicks playing recorders and inveighing against the pill. Perhaps future generations will amend the last verse of 'The Twelve Days of Christmas' to 'Twelve Gillicks Descending.'

Next morning the badgers, or a passing stray dog, will have upended Scarlett's dustbins and scattered Christmas left-overs all over the lawn.

Sales

Before the turkey is cold on the table, while we are still panicking about paying the Christmas debts we have run up, we are being inveigled by the media not only into booking our summer holidays – when there seems no hope that we will ever fit into a bikini again – but also into spending fortunes at the sales.

Last year, one man queued for eighteen days to be the first into the Selfridges sale on 27 December, where he bought a video recorder, a video camera, and a television set at a record low price. When Selfridges realised that he was giving the whole lot to charity, they kindly let him have them all at half the price.

In South Belfast, in overnight temperatures well below freezing point, people queued from Christmas Eve. The management generously hired a leading folk group to entertain the queue, and offered them free breakfast before the doors were opened at 9.30 a.m. on the 27th. The man at the front of the queue got a £349 video recorder for £9.

I suppose it's one way of spending Christmas and at least it must have stopped them watching television.

Thank-you letters

Not a Beecher's Brook at Christmas but definitely a rather hairy water-jump. Try and get thank-you letters written on Boxing Day or a dreadful paralysis sets in, and you get sliding-eyed teenagers home for half-term in February saying defensively, 'Well I definitely wrote, but your writing in the telephone book's so lousy that I may have read the address wrong.'

The upper classes, who are very hot on good manners, make even four-year-olds write letters: 'Thank you for my luvly prezent', plus a picture of a Christmas tree. To avoid tantrums in the nursery, this has usually been written by the nanny with her left hand.

If you chivvy older children too much, they get bolshy and won't even get halfway down the page by Twelfth Night. This is shaming when all one's much younger nephews and nieces write witty and charming letters that get three-quarters down a second page, and arrive on 28 December.

My husband's godson, who is at prep school, went to the other extreme and wrote all his letters before the end of the

Christmas term. His parents were astounded, until he showed
them the letters, which all had carefully spaced blanks to be
filled in on Boxing Day.

I had great difficulty this year stopping my son from
running his letters off on the word processor, thundering to
him that 'Thank you for your lovely *present*' is not specific
enough. Nor is it enough just to have thanked Granny when
she rang up on Christmas Day.

There was one dreadful year when I discovered that I'd
made my shopping list on the back of the children's thank-
you letters, which were still waiting on the kitchen shelf for
me to provide envelopes and addresses. And another, when I
primed my daughter, then ten, to put in a sentence to all
female relations, saying that she hoped Christmas hadn't
exhausted them too much. My daughter dutifully sat down at
the kitchen table, and in the middle of the first letter asked
my cockney char how to spell the word 'weren't', in the sentence, 'I hope you weren't too tired.'

'No such word,' said the char firmly, 'It's "wasn't" too tired.'

So my daughter 'wasn't-ed' all her letters, and later had to rewrite the whole lot.

Beware of protesting too much. If you rave on and on and on about the orange muffler knitted you by Rich Great Aunt Phyllis, you will get an orange jersey next year, orange mittens the year after that, and probably nothing but orange sheep left you in her will.

Beware, too, of truth. Some years ago, when it first became fashionable in London, I gave a vat of seeded mustard to my father-in-law for Christmas. Being a perfect gentleman, he wrote me a sweet letter saying how delighted he was, and how the mustard would enhance every meal. Next day I got a letter from my brother-in-law, who'd been staying with my father-in-law over Christmas, saying, 'Thank you for the Stilton – actually I hate the stuff, so I swapped it for Dad's mustard, because he can't stand that either.'

The pantomime

If you can't face it, go to *Peter Pan* instead, which is one of the best plays ever written, and which Granny adores because Captain Hook went to Eton.

Drinks parties

Christmas generally results in a spate of drinks with the locale, in which you stand about, easing your chilblained feet out of high heels, asphyxiated by everyone's toiletries, agreeing with grannies that you can't think how their daughters do it, as little satsumaholics charge out of control through your legs.

No one ever gets off with anyone at Boxing Day drinks, because everyone's wearing their new Christmas jerseys – in wildly unbecoming colours – so that Rich Great Aunt Phyllis who gave it them can see how thrilled they are with it. Instantly when they get home, the jersey is thrust back into its polythene bag because they 'want to keep it for best' but actually because they want to rush into Cheltenham tomorrow and change it.

Misanthropists always hold mulled wine or hot punch parties, because it gives them the perfect opportunity to stay in the kitchen stirring some vile brew and never circulate among the guests. Today you can even buy Glühwein ready made, and heat it up, which must be even more disgusting. The only time it's justified is as a first drink to warm people up on very cold days. When the roads are icy in the country, you get wives arriving at parties not only purple with cold but also with rage, because their husbands have insisted on driving the safer old Land Rover which has neither heating nor windows any more.

Sometimes you are invited round for drinks to meet people's parents. Noël seldom gets asked because he's inclined to get drunk and tell blue jokes to the mothers, and to irritate the fathers by accepting a third drink when there are unmistakable sounds from the kitchen of potatoes being noisily mashed.

Scarlett gets very embarrassed because Noël refuses to go to drinks with bores five miles away on the excuse that he might get breathalysed and lose his licence (he never minds if it's likely to be a good party). She then has to ring and say that Noël has flu, and invariably the hostess's sister on her way to the party apprehends him driving cheerfully up to the Dog and Trumpet.

Men, particularly those over forty, have an infuriating habit of getting you to parties hours early. How many times have I made up in the car, praying for red lights, and finally gouged my eye half out with a mascara wand; then on arrival seen, through the glass front door, my hostess coming downstairs, one eye made-up, frantically pulling out rollers, and lip-read the exasperated words: 'My God, are they here already!'

Men also tend to get a lot of word-of-mouth invitations at Christmas, mainly at parties or in pubs, when they've had a few, and get very confused about dates. Either you turn up for drinks, and after a lengthy recce, seeing no lights on and no cars arriving, slink home and change back into scruff order; or even worse, you knock on the door to be greeted by your host in scruff order, obviously having a cosy supper in front of the fire, who insists you come in for a drink, and you have to go through the same thing the following night.

If you invite country people to drinks in London, they will

'You are a pocket of loneliness and boredom
and I have come to break you up!'

arrive at noon, just when you're crawling out of bed. Conversely, people from London always turn up at country parties in fur coats at 1.30 p.m. just as the party's breaking up.

If you have a lot of people in for a drinks party, never judge its success by the roar of noise. People may simply not be able to hear one another. A host and hostess at any party must constantly police the room for pockets of loneliness and boredom, and break them up.

Teenage parties

After Boxing Day it's all juggling. Robin's godmother is coming for tea, Noël's sister and her lover are coming to lunch, along with a mother who's driving a hundred miles to bring her teenage daughter to stay with Holly for the pony club dance that night. Five other teenagers have to be met at Stroud at 2.40 p.m. A jolly local granny has been asked to supper to amuse Scarlett's mother, because Noël and Scarlett have to take Holly and Robin to the dance, but suddenly rings up to say that she can't make it because she's got to help behind the scenes and sheepdog the grandchildren at her own daughter's drinks party this evening. Noël had agreed to take Robin to Northampton to stay with a schoolfriend tomorrow – anything to get away from his mother-in-law who's decided to stay on for a few more days – but rats at the last moment because he's been asked shooting. Noël's mother-in-law is frightfully upset; she can't understand how Noël can be so snappy with her all the time, and so charming to his friends when they ring up.

The one salvation at this stage is to ask a really nice gay man to stay, who has no frightful children to fight with yours, who can take over cooking supper if need be or afford to take you out dinner, who always brings wonderful presents, who is a fund of anecdotes, and who gets on terribly well with Granny because she reminds him of his own mother.

If you have teenage children, you will spend the entire Christmas holidays changing sheets and making up beds as their friends drift in and out. Don't bother too much about clean sheets between teenagers. If they're going to a party, they seldom spend more than a couple of hours in bed anyway.

Get in a good supply of Erace – invariably someone has spots after all the Christmas chocolate – and several spare black ties, or even dress shirts – teenage boys invariably forget to bring them. My son always takes two to dances, in case one gets ripped off.

You will also have the thrill of thinking how distinguished your children look in their first dinner jackets, because both sexes wear them to parties these days, the only difference being that the girls roll back the sleeves.

Drive them to the dance – if it's private you will easily find the place because of the great disco roar issuing out of some house inappropriately called The Old Rectory. Don't stay. Teenagers are put in one room, wrinklies in another, and embarrass the hell out of their children by peering through the crack of the door to see how they are getting on, and occasionally rushing in, grabbing a teenager, thrusting her at their daughter and screaming, 'She knows Molly Piggott, darling,' or 'Juliet goes to Westonbirt, don't you play them at lacrosse?'

Equally, if you take your children to a dance in a public place, don't stay either. It will upset you if your children don't get off with anyone, but even more if they do. At the last teenage dance I went to, my daughter disappeared into a ballroom darker than Great Agrippa's inkwell for so long that my husband went to find her. He came back, white with rage, holding by the scruff of the neck my daughter, who was snarling and snapping like a Jack Russell that she Absolutely Hated Daddy.

'What was she doing?' I asked in alarm.

'She was sitting on two boys' knees,' came the reply.

Later, looking for my son, I found him sharing a half bottle of vodka, and a Havana cigar with one of his school-friends; and finally, groping round under the table for my bag, I found that the only two boys in our party who'd been behaving remotely well were holding hands with one another.

Children's parties

Only masochists have little children's parties at Christmas. Once a year on their birthday is more than enough for any child. In fact, sensible parents should take extra strong precautions in late March and early April, or even refrain from sexual intercourse altogether, so as not to produce a little Capricorn baby, who will require a specially big birthday party over the festive season to make up for not getting many presents because his birthday is so near Christmas.

I've been to a marvellous party

'We give parties,' wrote Frank Muir, 'because we are parting ourselves from feelings of guilt that people have had us round to their place, and we haven't had them back; and having them in one fell swoop is easier than two by two.'

Or, as a neighbour said delightfully last Christmas, 'Do come to drinks before lunch on 28 December – I'm asking all the people I can't face having to dinner.'

I always adore the idea of giving a Christmas party, romantically envisaging roaring fires, hundreds of scarlet candles, and all my friends looking beautiful in velvet and lots of glitter; but I feel very strongly that everyone should think very coolly and very seriously before embarking on one. It's all great fun, sending out invitations early in December, and having the excitement of the replies swelling the Christmas card post. But when you're utterly knackered after Christmas and a hundred people are suddenly due for dinner on 4 January, you may well find that you have neither the heart, the energy and certainly not the cash to entertain them – and the victuals you have to prepare to feed your five thousand may turn out to be the last cheese straws that break the camel's back.

For a party at another time of the year, you can generally expect a 70–75 per cent acceptance; but at Christmas, with everyone bringing their house guests, and their Aged Parents, and their children because they can't get a babysitter (why the hell the Aged Ps can't babysit I can never understand), and all the spare men bringing their new ladies, it's a very different story. We asked a 100 to a lunch party one New

Year's Day and ended up with 140 per cent acceptance. People
are probably so fed up with cooking at Christmas that they'll
go anywhere for a free meal.

Friends sometimes ask you if you're going to be away at
Christmas, then when you say yes, say, in tones of colossal
relief, 'Oh *what* a shame – we were going to ask you to a
party.'

A far more sensible idea is to have your party in early
December, so that you'll get lots of invitations over Christmas;
or in late February or March, when it'll be really appreciated
because people need cheering up.

If you are committed to giving a party at Christmas,
telephone, or write a letter. Don't send out invitations, or
you'll have the hideous embarrassment of going to someone
else's drinks party, where your invitation is up on the mantelpiece, and having to talk glazedly to scores of beady people
whom you should have invited.

Invite a mixture of those you love and those you owe and
ask lots of pretty people – a party needs sex appeal. Some
people nobly hand over their houses for the night so that their
teenage children can have their own party unimpeded. I think
this is insanity. You may trust your own children not to break
the place up, but you can't rely on other people's. Anyway at
Christmas it's more fun to ask all ages, but do draw the line at
the very young or very boring old people. The former constantly distract their parents or get dumped on other guests;
and there's nothing worse than being stuck on the sofa with
someone's turgid geriatric mother, particularly when her
daughter, when you're finally released after a three-hour stint,
says, 'I knew you'd enjoy Mummy – isn't she a gem?'

Keep the food simple. You can have a very good party on
kedgeree, sausages and mash, or moussaka. Offer people
straight red or white. Cocktails take far too long to mix, and
mulled wine, as well as being disgusting, is too complicated to
keep hot.

If it's an evening party and you're going to play loud music,
ask or warn the near neighbours; and, bearing in mind the
knackered housewife's overweight eyelids, keep the lighting
soft. Start the house off warm, but constantly police the
temperature.

Here is a typical Christmas party. Noël, determined to keep
things simple, has ordered curry from the local Indian
takeaway, and told Scarlett not to fuss around with any salads.
There is mutiny without any bounty over the guest list.

'You haven't asked *Tristram Piggott*!' storm Holly and Robin.
'He's a wimp – none of our friends will speak to him.'

As more and more people accept, Scarlett smuggles in extra
supplies – to no avail. With hordes of visiting teenagers, the
red apples for the Waldorf salad go in a morning, and several
pounds of grapes, intended for a pudding, are reduced to
hedgehogs of stalks overnight.

There's a tricky moment when Noël catches Scarlett in the
pantry about to make mayonnaise for some closet coleslaw.

'Bottled will do,' he says firmly.

Meekly Scarlett concurs; the road to Hellmann's is paved
with good intentions.

Party day dawns; the rooms are cleared. On Noël's instructions, the daily removes the ornaments from all the surfaces,
but the house looks so awful that Scarlett puts them all back
again. In a desperate attempt to force them out, she has put
the indoor hyacinths in the hot cupboard.

Holly's sole contribution to the party is to drift in to
the kitchen at midday in her nightie, say it's naff to have spoons
with curry and everyone will expect pudding, and drift
out again. All Scarlett's hints about Holly looking so nice
'in your Laura Ashley, darling' fall on deaf, if newly pierced,
ears. Holly is hell bent on wearing Scarlett's new backless
black.

Despite Noël's claim that even numbers don't matter,
Scarlett is fretting about the shortage of spare men. Some girl
rings up to cancel.

'Oh goodee, I mean oh gosh, how sad,' says Scarlett, 'We
MUST get together in the New Year.'

Zero hour. The house is radiant with candles; the carpets
stretch out, virginal. Fortunately, between parties, memory
blots out the sheer terror that always grips her before everyone
arrives, when all Scarlett craves is a quadruple vodka laced
with Valium which would lay her out for ever. Outside, Robin
and his mates, already blue with cold, wait stamping their
feet, to help park the cars.

Then everyone starts arriving in a rush, eager for drinks and introductions, which Scarlett knows one must do properly, giving people a slight lead: 'This is Fiona: she's a tower of strength at the local Distressed Gentlefolk', or 'This is Charlie, who's just bought Badger Hall.'

It's obvious, too, that even numbers do matter. In one room is a surplus of beautiful women in the 30–40 age-group, who find being squeezed by Noël not *quite* enough. In another, a surplus of ravishing teenage boys with rooster hair, stand about having 'When d'you go back,/next week/lucky sod, I go back on Monday and I've got mocks' conversations with one another.

Matters are not helped when a mother expected to bring three exquisite teenage daughters turns up saying that they've all gone skiing with their father; nor when Holly and all her teenage friends take fright and bolt themselves into her bedroom.

'Don't be anti-social,' screams Scarlett, like Wee Willy Wrinkly, through the lock.

She is also very tight-lipped because Ms Stress, having been asked by Noël, who never got round to telling Scarlett, has just rolled up with her ghastly gay husband, Gordon, and two boot-faced children, followed by a whole busload of Noël's cronies from the Dog and Trumpet. There's no way the food's going to last out.

Success at last! One of Scarlett's forty-year-old girlfriends is nose to nose with a beautiful youth with an earring in his left ear. Despite the children telling her hundreds of times, Scarlett can't remember whether left or right means that you're gay. She does hope her friend isn't squandering her wiles on a wrong-sided earring.

Scarlett knows that you're not expected to enjoy your own parties – just act as an unpaid waitress and rescue people whose eyes are beginning to glaze out of drink or boredom – but this one is quite out of control, and Noël says that they can't eat for at least ten minutes. The place seems so much more crowded with all those padded shoulders and there's a yelling bottleneck in the hall, where people are fighting their way into the next room to see if it's more exciting, and, finding it isn't, fighting their way back again. Scarlett's introduced

everyone to everyone, and people are beginning to put their
hands over their glasses, and say 'I'll fall over if I don't eat.'
Difficult Patch is in the hot cupboard with the hyacinths.

Upstairs are scenes of Petronian debauchery, with necking
teenagers, their braces locking, occupying every bed and sofa. At
least they're too busy devouring each other to want any dinner.

Thank God, it's ready at last. Everyone else swarms into
the kitchen and tucks into the curry. Most of the salads go
too, but not the cheese which Scarlett panic-bought in
Cirencester that morning. She must remember in future that
no one eats Stilton at parties unless you provide Gold Spot or
Polos for pudding.

The most frequent request now is for glasses of water because the curry is so hot, and for kitchen roll as another glass
of red wine is kicked over on the carpet.

Music is now pounding out of Noël's study. The next hurdle
is getting people to dance. After food, they tend to sit around
for an hour – like not swimming after lunch.

Teenage boys keep coming up to Scarlett and saying, 'Holly
has asked me to stay the night.' 'No no no', screams Scarlett
hysterically.

At least they're dancing now. But still the generations in-
hibit each other.

'Don't watch us,' grumbles Holly as Scarlett peers into the
darkened room to see if she or Robin are getting off with
anyone.

Later, however, circling dreamily in the muscular arms of
the local cricket captain, Scarlett opens her eyes, and through
the fireflies of illicit teenage cigarettes sees Holly and her best
friends giggling at her in mock disapproval.

Explaining afterwards that the cricket captain was 'just
something to hang on to when one is tired, like the strap in
the tube', doesn't wash either.

Noël and Ms Stress have been missing for hours; perhaps
they've joined Difficult Patch in the hot cupboard. One of Ms
Stress's boot-faced children is trying to murder the other with
one of the hired knives. And ghastly gay Gordon has been
chatting up Robin for much too long.

By 2.00 a.m. the party is fragmenting. Scarlett doesn't even
mind that the only thing she's run out of is salt, which now

'Oh, sorry!'

lies like patches of snow over the wine stains on the carpet.

At 5.00 a.m., Noël, a hard core of teenagers, and sundry drunks from the Dog and Trumpet are playing Twenty-one Aces. Scarlett collapses into bed. Did she dream it, or did she really hear Holly joyfully screaming that Daddy's just eaten two Bonios?

Surfacing four hours later, she finds several pale teenage boys who seem to have stayed the night after all.

'Sorry they're weren't enough girls for you,' says Scarlett.

'Oh, it was a great party,' they chorus. 'Alastair was sick, Henry was sick, so was Marcus, and Anthony and the Jones boys.'

Scarlett thanks God that Robin's going back to school next week to dry out.

Some of the silver seems to be missing, too.

'The night of the short knives,' says Noël.

Scarlett faints when she peers round the door of Holly's room and finds the floor littered with broken glass, fag ends, 20 empty bottles, 15 cups, Scarlett's backless dress, and Difficult Patch finishing up the half eaten plates of curry.

At least the mess is confined to one room. Shutting the door firmly, Scarlett concentrates on the wonderful selection of scarves, gloves and coats that have been left behind by departing drunks; and there are still all the party thank-you letters to look forward to.

Five: We Make the Golden Journey to Samarkand

Christmas Abroad

One alternative to all this is to cop out of Christmas altogether and spend it in a hotel or abroad. This is fine if you can accept the fact that – like people who went to America in the war – you will be made to feel desperately guilty that at a time of national emergency you are thinking only of yourself.

Your mother-in-law, for a start, will say huffily: 'Of course I can manage all on my own; off you both go to Kenya and enjoy yourselves.'

Girlfriends will display undisguised envy: 'Gosh, you're lucky – no cooking or washing up. I wish *we* could afford a break like that.'

Bear in mind that the break itself may not be as marvellous as you expect. Remember all those gleeful accounts in the national press before Christmas, about Britons travelling abroad facing chaos and delays because of airport strikes, congested car parks at Heathrow, cross-channel ferry disputes, hovercraft services disrupted by bad weather, not to mention thirteen-mile traffic tailbacks from Dover to Canterbury. Someone should write a cautionary Christmas story called 'The Canterbury Tailback'.

It is also crucial to make a recce of the hotel abroad beforehand. The January papers are crammed with stories headlined 'Heartbreak Hotel', in which pensioners, having blued their savings on Xmas in Tenerife, find rubble in the pathway, no roof on the dining-room, bare electric wires hanging from bedroom walls, disgusting food, and pneumatic drilling twenty-four hours a day – which must be even worse than grandchildren.

Tragedy comes too from high expectation. P. J. Kavanagh, dreaming of a white Christmas in a congenial and convivial Swiss chalet, found very little snow, modern barracks architecture, and midnight mass in a huge hall like a shop; and all the maids were Sloane Rangers, so he couldn't even practise his French on them.

Equally, if you expect to drive through France stopping at different hotels for long lunches and dinners, you will find that most restaurants close on 24 and 25 December if not for the whole of Christmas week, and that you have to book well ahead for both Christmas lunch and the *reveillon*. Bethlehem, which should be the ideal place to spend Christmas, is so excruciatingly commercial that a visit would turn any decent Christian atheist.

Christmas abroad or in a hotel could perhaps succeed for a married couple who are both working so hard at their careers that they need to spend some time alone together. It often works, too, for retired couples, who've made their pile, and don't want to impose on their families; or for a wife when her children are spending Christmas with the ex-husband – although if she chooses somewhere too exotic and takes her lover along too, she may find her alimony chopped in the New Year.

One family of six who'd sold their big house, and were cramped in the tiniest cottage, took off to Cyprus and Egypt this Christmas, and had a wonderful time: 'Lots of cheap drink and skiing,' said the teenage daughter, 'and my eldest brother gave me a camel ride as a Christmas present.'

Equally, Christmas could be fun abroad if you were staying with rich and very amusing people. Jonathan Routh in Jamaica wrote he was woken at 7.30 a.m. by the shriek of peacocks and carols with a reggae beat on the wireless. There followed a breakfast of pineapple, bacon and eggs, and smuggled-in bangers; then off to the beach, where goat curry was handed out to the poor of the island and Father Christmas arrived by raft with a sack of goodies.

Avoid at all costs spending Christmas in a hotel with little children, who need companions of their own age, who want their toys around them, and who get desperately bored if they're confined to a small space. If you stay in England, it's much too cold to take them to play on the beach, and if you go abroad – real shock horror – the television doesn't speak English.

Children hate long formal meals, and you can't tell them to get down in a hotel as they're likely to break the place up. One friend, spending Christmas in a chi-chi hotel in the Cotswolds, full of china ornaments and antique furniture, said that he didn't leave go of the scruffs of his children's necks for four days: 'It was like staying with my mother-in-law, but 100 per cent more expensive.'

If your children are frightened of the dark, you have to sit with them until they go to sleep. If you leave the door open and a light on in the passage (which goes off thirty seconds later anyway in France) your room will probably get burgled.

If you take teenagers away at Christmas, make sure again that you pick a hotel where there are other teenagers for them to get off with. School groups are forced by their teachers to stick together and not mix. Après-ski in the hotel disco can be isolated and lonely.

The thing people seem to miss most if they go away is a proper Christmas dinner. In English hotels you get mega-grumblings because of 'no proper trimmings – disgusting'. Abroad it can be even worse.

'Christmas dinner,' wrote a friend from Switzerland, 'was cooked by a Sloane Ranger chalet girl who claimed to have done a Cordon Bleu course. It was more Cordon Noir. I didn't have to carve the miserable turkey; it was off the bone as soon as I prodded it with a fork, and tasted like pale stringy biltong.

'The poor girl said she wasn't used to Swiss ovens, and went into a swift decline.'

Perhaps this is why P. J. Kavanagh and his family opted for a large fondue instead.

Ultimately Wassail does seem to run through English veins, whether it's soldiers serving overseas dying to get home to be with their families; or the lone English trio found erecting a plastic Christmas tree hung with silver bells under the blazing sun on Bondi beach as they ate their Christmas lunch of prawns and avocado salad; or the appalled amusement felt by some English friends staying in the Middle East when an official proclamation in the local paper announced that 'Christmas is cancelled.'

Christmas has been compared to pregnancy and giving birth; but spent abroad it seems to have the disappointment and anti-climax of the Caesarian. For better or worse, we feel we can't truly appreciate it unless we suffer all the awful shopping, cooking and anti-climax at the time to produce it.

Left-overs

New Year's Eve

A ghastly hype. For some extraordinary reason, people, particularly those who are unmarried, believe that they have utterly failed socially if they aren't asked anywhere on New Year's Eve. In fact, they would be far more sensible to go to bed early with a good book. If you go out, mini cabs are double fare; you're liable to get your house burgled and yourself mugged or raped; and the entire police force is lurking in bushes waiting to catch home-going motorists.

If you feel compelled to give a New Year's Eve party, don't invite people to arrive too early or they'll go off the boil before midnight. Nine o'clock to nine thirty is about right, which will give them time to have a few drinks and dinner before you gather them all into one room to celebrate the passing of the old year. Do put on the radio at midnight with all speakers blaring, so that everyone can hear the chimes of Big Ben, and start kissing everyone else's wives and husbands and generally behaving badly.

A girlfriend summed up the whole thing. Just as midnight finished striking, and we were all happily knocking back champagne, from a dark corner she could be heard muttering, 'Bloody January again.'

Twelfth Night

At home poor Scarlett is slowly ploughing through a vast mountain of ironing, because the children all go back to school next week. She has put the Christmas decorations back in their box, and the tree outside the back door (it seemed such a shame to burn it when it had given them such pleasure) and swept up the pine needles.

She dreads taking down the Christmas cards, because it makes the sitting-room look so drab and colourless. If only she hadn't spent so much on Christmas they could afford to brighten it up with new curtains or at least new cushions. Later she's got to pack up and post back to Petersfield the gloves, boots and quilted hot-water bottle that Granny left behind, omitting to point out that Difficult Patch has punctured the hot-water bottle.

Upstairs, above the pounding surf beat of Robin's record player, she can hear Nicholas and little Carol screaming at each other. Nor can she expect any help in packing the trunks from Holly, who is locked in her room, reduced to the depths of misanthropy by mugging up St Luke for mock O-levels.

Scarlett feels depressed. Sadly she no longer has the excuse that it's still Christmas to justify the midday nip (a treble vodka and tonic) to keep her going; all the parties are over, and she's already broken her New Year's resolution to lose weight. Christmas, with all its faults, was a break in the monotony of life. But at least she's her own boss, unlike poor Noël, who today went back to the relentless treadmill of the office; and who now, unknown to Scarlett, is roughing it at the Ritz over a three-hour lunch with Ms Stress, trying to piece together who it was that he mauled or insulted at the office party before Christmas.

If only, muses Scarlett, one could have Christmas every five years, then it would really be something to look forward to, like a royal wedding, and she and Noël wouldn't be almost bankrupted every January. If they could give up both drink *and* Christmas they'd be quite well off.

Her reverie is interrupted by little Carol howling down the stairs that Nicholas has decapitated her new Christmas doll, because she'd managed to wipe all his computer games.

'Never mind,' says Scarlett comfortingly, 'it's only 353 days until next Christmas.'